ONE-HOUR SHAKESPEARE: THE EARLY COMEDIES AND ROMANCES

The *One-Hour Shakespeare* series is a collection of abridged versions of Shakespeare's plays, designed specifically to accommodate both small and large casts.

This volume, *The Early Comedies and Romances*, includes the following plays:

- *A Midsummer Night's Dream*
- *Two Gentlemen of Verona*
- *The Tempest*
- *The Winter's Tale*

These accessible and versatile scripts are supported by: an introduction with emphasis on the evolution of the series and the creative process of editing; the One-Hour projects in performance, a chapter on implementing money-saving ideas and suggestions for production, whether in or outside a classroom setting; specific lesson plans to incorporate these projects successfully into an academic course; and cross-gender casting suggestions. These supplementary materials make the plays valuable not only for actors, directors and professors, but for any environment, cast or purpose.

Ideal for both academics and professionals, *One-Hour Shakespeare* is the perfect companion to teaching and staging the most universally read and performed playwright in history.

Julie Fain Lawrence-Edsell is an actress, director and Associate Professor of BFA Acting at the Pace School of Performing Arts, Pace University, New York. Some of her credits include: *The Last* (2019), *Concussion* (Sundance 2013), *Madam Secretary*, *Law & Order: SVU & CI*, *Kidnapped*, *Six Degrees*, *Third Watch*, *All My Children* and over a dozen Shakespearean productions.

One-Hour Shakespeare

The *One-Hour Shakespeare* series is a collection of abridged versions of Shakespeare's plays, designed specifically to accommodate both small and large casts. These accessible and versatile scripts are supported by: an introduction with emphasis on the evolution of the series and the creative process of editing; the One-Hour projects in performance, a chapter on implementing money saving ideas and suggestions for production whether in or outside of a classroom setting; specific lesson plans to incorporate these projects successfully into an academic course; and cross-gender casting suggestions. Ideal for both academics and professionals, *One-Hour Shakespeare* is the perfect companion to teaching and staging the most universally read and performed playwright in history.

One-Hour Shakespeare
The Comedies
Julie Fain Lawrence-Edsell

One-Hour Shakespeare
The Early Comedies and Romances
Julie Fain Lawrence-Edsell

One-Hour Shakespeare
The Tragedies
Julie Fain Lawrence-Edsell

One-Hour Shakespeare
The Tragicomedies
Julie Fain Lawrence-Edsell

For more information about this series, please visit: https://www.routledge.com/One-Hour-Shakespeare/book-series/1HS

ONE-HOUR SHAKESPEARE

The Early Comedies and Romances

Julie Fain Lawrence-Edsell

LONDON AND NEW YORK

First published 2020
by Routledge
2 Park Square, Milton Park, Abingdon, Oxon OX14 4RN

and by Routledge
52 Vanderbilt Avenue, New York, NY 10017

Routledge is an imprint of the Taylor & Francis Group, an informa business

© 2020 Julie Fain Lawrence-Edsell

The right of Julie Fain Lawrence-Edsell to be identified as author of this work has been asserted by her in accordance with sections 77 and 78 of the Copyright, Designs and Patents Act 1988.

All rights reserved. No part of this book may be reprinted or reproduced or utilised in any form or by any electronic, mechanical, or other means, now known or hereafter invented, including photocopying and recording, or in any information storage or retrieval system, without permission in writing from the publishers.

Trademark notice: Product or corporate names may be trademarks or registered trademarks, and are used only for identification and explanation without intent to infringe.

British Library Cataloguing-in-Publication Data
A catalogue record for this book is available from the British Library

Library of Congress Cataloging-in-Publication Data
A catalog record has been requested for this book

ISBN: 978-0-367-20637-6 (hbk)
ISBN: 978-0-367-20639-0 (pbk)
ISBN: 978-0-429-26264-7 (ebk)

Typeset in Bembo
by Newgen Publishing UK

CONTENTS

Acknowledgments vii

1 Introduction 1

2 One-Hour projects in performance: money-saving suggestions to consider with a minimal budget 3

3 Lesson plan and editing exercise 14

4 Cross-gender casting suggestions 17

5 A Midsummer Night's Dream 19

6 A Midsummer Night's Dream: suggested cast list and character assignments for a small cast 75

7 Two Gentlemen of Verona 76

8 Two Gentlemen of Verona: suggested cast list and character assignments for a small cast 136

9 The Tempest 137

10 The Tempest: suggested cast list and character assignments for a small cast 195

11 The Winter's Tale 196

12 The Winter's Tale: suggested cast list and character
    assignments for a small cast 255

ACKNOWLEDGMENTS

There are so many individuals and groups who have provided inspiration and support to me for this series over the years. Below, I would like to acknowledge and give very special thanks to a handful of individuals for going above and beyond with love, support, encouragement and guidance.

Dr. John Fain Lawrence and Emily Lawrence,
John, Jared and Owen Edsell,
Susan Lawrence,
Lynne Lawrence,
Jayme Barrett,
Julie Wolfson,
Matt Burnett,
Morgan Jenness,
Thomas Keith,
Catherine Sheehy,

and countless professors and students at the Pace School of Performing Arts.

1
INTRODUCTION

Shakespeare was my first love. I remember growing up, my family would pile into our old Dodge station wagon and drive 12 hours up the California coast to the Oregon Shakespeare Festival. There we would pitch a tent at the KOA campground and, come rain or shine, watch seven provocative plays in five days. This annual pilgrimage hooked me on William Shakespeare by the time I was 11 years old.

For the past 25 years, I've been successfully working in the entertainment industry as an actor, director and independent film producer and, since 2012, as a Professor of Acting at Pace University, the School of Performing Arts in New York City. At the university, my specialty is scene study with classical texts and the highlight for my students are the accessible *One-Hour Shakespeare* projects I've successfully implemented as lesson plans.

These personal edits and abridged versions of Shakespeare's classics are a perfect length for academic and professional productions and are designed specifically to accommodate small casts (5–8 actors), if you choose, or casts as numerous as the character count is in each play. There are suggestions of double and triple casting and, in some cases, character lines have been combined and some characters have been omitted. Acting companies and students can take these one-hour versions and perform them with or without production resources and still reap the benefits of the magnificent plays of William Shakespeare.

My creative process for editing these plays of Shakespeare down to an hour is first based on paying respect to the original text, rhythm, meter and through-line of the main characters in each play. I use multiple editions of each play to refer to throughout the editing process; The Arden Shakespeare, The Oxford Shakespeare, the Folger Shakespeare Library editions, The New Cambridge editions, The Pelican Shakespeare, The Signet classics, The Riverside Shakespeare, The Folio Society editions and The Complete Works of William Shakespeare online at http://shakespeare.mit.edu. Each editor takes a license with punctuation and the endings of words ("ed" or "'d") as well as many other word endings and spellings. I take the same license when editing the full text down to an hour. There are inconsistencies and variations on words, punctuation and formatting throughout all editions of Shakespeare's plays in print based on editorial choices and on whether an editor is using the First Folio or one of the Quarto versions as their source.

Each play in this collection includes line numbers and selected definitions. The line numbers will not correspond to the original line numbers in the full text of each play with the exception of the very beginning of each scene. Line numbers are included for easy reference during study and rehearsals. In regard to word definitions, I encourage actors and educators to use the *Shakespeare Lexicon and Quotation Dictionary* (Volumes I and II) by Alexander Schmidt, Dover Publications Inc., which does identify words by play, act, scene and original line numbers. It's an invaluable resource and what I used for all definitions in this series.

Each one-hour play in the collection has been performance vetted by members of the 2015–2018 BFA Acting classes of The School of Performing Arts at Pace University, NYC.

Please enjoy the accessibility of these personal edits, in-performance production suggestions, lesson plans and cast list suggestions. My hope is that these projects will ultimately inspire actors, audiences and educators alike to then pick up the complete text of each play and engage in Shakespeare more fully.

2
ONE-HOUR PROJECTS IN PERFORMANCE

Money-saving suggestions to consider with a minimal budget

Shakespeare's plays have proven successful in performance, time and time again, set in any time period and any location. This provides a great deal of artistic freedom and creativity when considering how you will structure your projects. Some fundamental production ideas to consider are what your theatre space will look like, where it will be, whether you will have access to lighting equipment, whether you will have access to scenery or basic furniture and what design choices you will make for costumes and sound.

Theatre space

Any room or area, inside or outside, can be made into a performance space. The "playing space" or stage is defined by where the audience is placed, choice of entrances and exits, and any scenery and lighting available. Some spaces to consider might include the following.

Traditional theatre space

This space is already defined, often with a raised stage and a proscenium arch, but you have the choice to use entrances and exits through the audience aisles as well as the on-stage wings.

Black Box theatre or any classroom or multi-purpose room

The space can be defined in multiple ways; traditional (sometimes referred to as proscenium; Figure 1), a thrust stage (Figure 2), a traverse stage which has a center alley for the playing space (Figure 3) or theatre in the round (Figures 4 and 5).

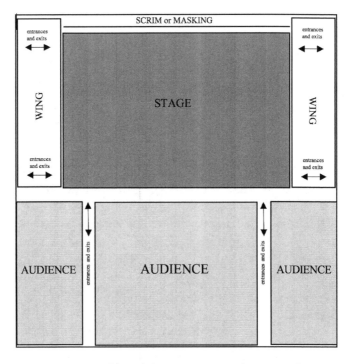

FIGURE 1 Traditional theatre space – audience out front

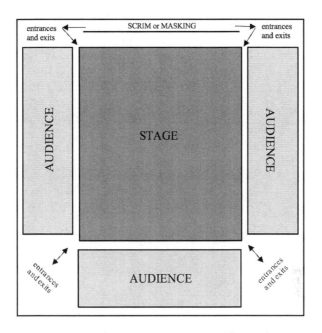

FIGURE 2 Thrust stage – seating on three sides

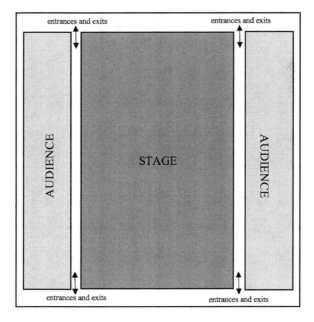

FIGURE 3 Traverse stage – audience on opposite sides

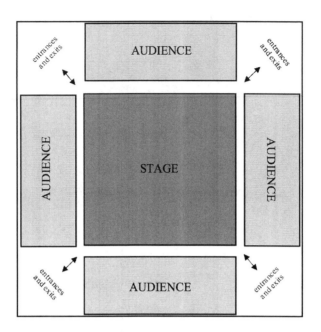

FIGURE 4 Theatre in the round – audience on all sides

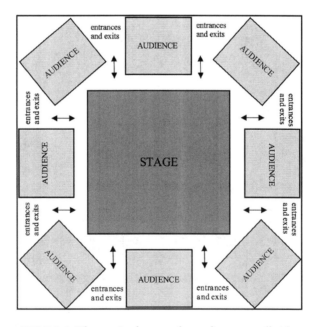

FIGURE 5 Theatre in the round – audience on all sides

Outdoor area

These spaces are limitless. Some areas to consider might include a quad or green space of a campus, a park, a private garden, a rooftop, an area of a beach, etc. The same principle of defining the space for a black box theater can be used here. Where do you want your audience? Where is your "playing space"?

Outdoor environments cannot be as easily controlled as a traditional or indoor theatre space due to lights and sounds. There may be birds, insects, rabbits, honking cars, planes flying overhead, loud voices and the weather to contend with. However, all of these environmental factors can create fantastic and spontaneous in-the-moment performance opportunities, which can be thrilling for actors and audiences alike.

Site specific areas

These spaces provide excellent and, sometimes, more controlled environments for a "playing space" depending on the specific site chosen. Permission to use the space may need to be granted, if the space is private. There is no limit to what one may consider a performance space. Some specific ideas to consider are:

- A small intimate library or the corner of a larger one to suggest the locations in *Measure for Measure* (Angelo's office, a prison cell, Isabella's place of worship, etc.). If you have access to a place of worship this could be a provocative and powerful location to choose.
- A school cafeteria, indoor or outdoor, to suggest a busy market place, the Rialto, the public court and other locales in *The Merchant of Venice*.
- A campground and its surroundings or a barnyard, stables and accompanying bales of hay to suggest the Forest of Arden and all locations in *As You Like It*.
- A park with benches and walkways to suggest the environments for *A Midsummer Night's Dream*.
- A green area adjacent to or in sight of a graveyard for *Hamlet* or even *Macbeth*. In one of the many film versions of *Hamlet*, the director chose to make Denmark the name of a corporation where Claudius works and not the country where Hamlet lives. The site-specific space used for many scenes was a Wall Street office building.
- The grand steps of a building to suggest the various locations of Rome in *Julius Caesar* (ancient Rome, the Senate, the Capital, an open Forum, etc.).
- Private walking gardens for *Much Ado About Nothing*.
- A courtyard surrounded by multi-level buildings (school buildings or apartments with a useable window), a structure with a front porch or an

interior of a building with a staircase landing for the aloft scenes and all else in *Romeo and Juliet*.
- A futbol pitch or practice fields (from the 18-yard line through to the frame of the goal) to suggest the environments for *Two Gentlemen of Verona*. Valentine and Proteus can be two gentlemen "V"arsity athletes.
- A plot of beach for *The Tempest*.

Entrances and exits

Entrances and exits for the actors can be through the right and left wings both upstage and downstage in the traditional space, through any aisles in the audience, around the right or left corner areas of audience seats, upstage center of the stage space if there is masking hung which has a center separation or upstage far left and far right around masking if masking or a scrim is being used (entrance and exit options are pictured in Figures 1–5). Actors can also choose to have chairs placed on stage or in the audience and use those as their entrance and exit positions.

Defining your space

Once a space has been decided on, you have chosen how to configure the audience seating and you defined specific entrances and exits that the actors will use, here are some additional money-saving suggestions to consider:

- Hang a dark or light sheet (masking/scrim) upstage center to serve as an area for slide projections and/or an offstage area for quick changes. A whiteboard on rollers is convenient to use as well. Additionally, you may choose to use more than one scrim to create walls if that is desired;
- Define your offstage area. Offstage can be behind the audience seating, behind masking or a scrim or in the wings if using a traditional theatre space. You might also decide not to designate an offstage space and allow the actors to be seen at all times. If this is your choice, a suggestion would be to have chairs or acting blocks placed in a semi-circle towards the upstage area of the playing space or in two rows opposite one another on the sides of the playing space for the actors to sit in when they are "offstage" and not in a particular scene. The actors' bodies then frame the playing space as well;
- If using slides or projected images to further suggest the environment for each scene, either a rear projector or a front projector can work. The placement of the projector will dictate the blocking or staging of the

scenes. Rear projectors can allow for an actor in the ensemble to operate, when behind the masking, and will not constrict the blocking of scenes on stage and in front of the masking. Projectors are often available to sign out through Media departments in schools and universities;
- Basic acting cubes (standard furniture for a black-box or studio space), chairs and A-frame ladders can be used to further define the setting for each scene and serve as the "scenery" (a throne, seats, a table, a bed, rocks to hide behind, a balcony, a pulpit, a cave, the bow of a ship, the entrance to a castle, etc.);
- Basic props, supplied by actors or a school prop collection, can consist of whatever you feel is essential to tell the story of the scene (stage knives, stage blood, wine glasses, flashlights, safe candles, fighting implements, flowers, letters, books, food, etc.).

Lighting

This will be determined by what is available in the space and whether the chosen space is inside or outside. Without a budget set aside for lighting, here are some suggestions:

- If your theatre space is inside you can choose to have the house lights turned fully on or off. If your chosen theatre space is outside then your options are daylight, dusk or evening moonlight;
- With the house lights on, the audience as well as the actors are illuminated which can provide great opportunities for direct address and audience involvement;
- When house lights are turned off then clip lights, portable work lights and flashlights can be used to illuminate the playing space and actor's bodies and provide ambience by creating shadows and adding a sense of mystery and danger. A "ghost light" or footlights (if available) can help further define the space;
- Cellphone lights are also a convenient choice, easily accessible and readily moved around the stage by the actors;
- Safe candles placed at the perimeter of the audience or stage may add to the ambience. There are practical uses for safe candles as props as well (*Macbeth, Othello, Hamlet, Julius Caesar, Two Gentlemen of Verona, Measure for Measure, Romeo and Juliet, A Midsummer Night's Dream*, etc.);
- If your chosen performance space is outside and the performance is during the evening then portable work lights, tiki torches (safely managed), flashlights, cellphone lights and safe candles are all practical choices.

Sound

Live or recorded music and ambient noises can help augment scene changes and add to the mood of the project as well as set the tone for each scene. Below are suggestions to consider without a budget:

- A soundscape and music tracks can be created and mixed by the ensemble of actors using Logic Pro, Garage Band, iTunes playlists or any other program the actors are comfortable with. The created sound design can then be played on QLab or other familiar programs during the performance by offstage actors or a volunteer who is not in the project. A wi-fi speaker is also a practical choice.
    - It has been my experience that young artists are much more adept at seeking out advances in technology in regard to listening, recording and playing music. There may be other computer programs that work as well as the ones that I have mentioned.
- Live music can be played by the ensemble of actors (guitar, ukulele, drums, piano (if available), portable keyboards, small percussion instruments, etc.) whether the play defines those characters as musicians or not. Some suggestions to consider for music playing characters are:
    - The Fairies and the Mechanicals in *A Midsummer Night's Dream*;
    - Bertram wooing Diana or Parolles with his "drum" in *All's Well That Ends Well*;
    - Amiens, Silvius, the Lords and Hymen in *As You Like It*;
    - Feste the clown in *Twelfth Night*;
    - Ophelia in *Hamlet*;
    - Lucius in *Julius Caesar*;
    - Moth in *Love's Labour's Lost*;
    - The Witches, Lady Macduff and her son in *Macbeth*;
    - Claudio in *Measure for Measure*;
    - Claudio in *Much Ado About Nothing*;
    - Lorenzo and Balthazar in *The Merchant of Venice*;
    - Ariel in *The Tempest*;
    - Valentine in *Two Gentleman of Verona*;
    - Romeo, Mercutio and the Nurse in *Romeo and Juliet*;
    - Time/Chorus in *The Winter's Tale*.

Costumes

If a costume shop is available to you for borrowing specific items gratis then you ideally will want to select items that fall within a general time frame.

Simple costumes tend to allow for more ease with quick changes and, in a small cast production with double and triple casting, quick changes are plentiful. If borrowing from a costume shop is not an option for you then below are some simple costume ideas to consider:

- Actors can wear a neutral clothing-base – basic black pants, shirts, skirts and shoes to create a clean silhouette. Other colors may serve as your neutral too but black and/or white seems to present the fewest variations in hues;
- Add one piece of simple clothing, with color, to accessorize the neutral base and help distinguish between the multiple characters each actor plays. Once this is established then the audience will immediately associate the clothing item with the specific character. Simple clothing choices might consist of coats, jackets, vests, scarves, hats, shirts, aprons, capes, etc. Belts can double as sword and weapon holders if there are weapons carried. Suggested clothing uses include:
  - White, beige and/or blue button-up shirts for messengers;
  - Colored skirts for female characters;
  - Structured hats or camoflauge items for kings, generals, soldiers;
  - Vests for female characters dressing as male characters (Viola in *Twelfth Night*, Julia in *Two Gentlemen of Verona*, Rosalind in *As You Like It*);
  - Capes and robes for supernatural characters, soothsayers, Friars and Priests;
  - Baseball caps worn backward or forward or bandanas for youthful characters;
  - Tailored scarves or cardigans for male or female characters of a higher status;
  - Particolored fabric remnants for clowns and jesters.

Switching from character to character

- Quick changes can occur in sight of the audience, if the ensemble chooses, or behind the upstage masking, the audience seating or any other designated offstage area. The changes will often be fast paced and require that as soon as an actor exits the stage they will turn around and quickly enter as a new character with a different accessory (hat, scarf, vest, jacket) as well as a new point of view, body language, rhythm and voice if they choose.
- Letting the audience in on "the magic of theatre" and quick character changes is a provocative idea to play with and can lead to fruitful

discoveries in rehearsal. Implementing them in performance comes down to a personal choice for the actors and director of the project. Allowing the audience to see the changes occurring and watch an actor assume another character in full view can lead to a deeper appreciation of the actor's art and requires the audience to further activate their own imaginations. This can successfully be achieved with quick changes off-stage as well.

An additional note on quick changes: the plays have all been edited to accommodate actors playing multiple characters who may, in the full-length play, be on stage together at the same time. To manage this traffic pattern, in some cases, lines have been reassigned to other characters, or additional exits and entrances have been created. These allow for an actor to make a character/costume change and then "re-enter" and engage in the same scene as a different character. If you desire to have all characters in the scene remain on stage together or the scene requires all characters on stage and you are limited by a small cast, a suggestion is to use a coat rack as a "stand-in." The rack can be draped with the costume accessory for your character of choice to suggest they are still on stage and listening. This can also be achieved by placing the costume accessory on the ground or on a chair on stage or by using a hand puppet as a "stand in." This same concept can be used to encourage comedic or "slapstick" moments. For example, in *Twelfth Night*, if limited by a small cast, the actor playing Antonio will also be assigned to play Sir Toby and, in Act III scene IV, they will have a sword fight with one another! This is highly entertaining for the audience and can add to the comedy in an already comedic play.

Deciding on a time period

The date, time period and location (country, city) for the projects will be suggested by choices in music, use of costumes, slides projected and accents and dialects used. Most projects I have seen have not specified a time and place but create a general sense of a modern world sometime within the last 50 years. These are highly successful and place more focus on the text and character development. That being said, some more specific ideas of time periods/locations that I have seen successfully implemented are:

- The world of Harry Potter for *Romeo and Juliet*. All sword fights were done with magic wands and sound effects, a use of the "invisibility cloak" for Romeo in the "Balcony scene" and suggestions with the Apothecary and the cordials/vials;

- The American 1950s with hoop skirts accentuating the female form, red lips and rockabilly clothes and music for the men for *Measure for Measure*;
- Film Noir with an Italian influence for *Much Ado About Nothing*;
- Contemporary wartime early 2000s for *Julius Caesar*;
- Modern day wartime after 2010 for *All's Well That Ends Well*;
- Northeast, USA, boarding school atmosphere for *Two Gentlemen of Verona*.

<u>Choices are limitless! HAVE FUN!!!</u>

3
LESSON PLAN AND EDITING EXERCISE

Objective – students will work with their assigned ensemble of actors/classmates and use six weeks of class time to rehearse, memorize, stage and finally perform their projects. Students will be asked to incorporate techniques from past acting classes, voice classes, speech classes, stage combat and movement classes.

I divide each section (two of them, approximately 10–16 students) into two equal groups and assign each group a play. I provide casting for all roles.

Each week the students have three designated hours of rehearsals during their scheduled class time, which I facilitate and observe, and they are required to schedule at least two full company rehearsals outside of class each week and other individual scene rehearsals.

Lesson plan as it appears in my syllabus given to students
One-Hour Shakespeare projects – requirements

I will divide the class into two equal groups and assign each group a Shakespearean play. I will also assign roles. Some double and triple casting may occur.

- You will be responsible for additional edits to the one-hour version provided based on discoveries made in the rehearsal room which will require very close reading of the text, attention to the thru-line of each

character, a solid understanding of iambic pentameter, and attention to plot points both primary and secondary. You will choose what to keep in the final text and what to edit out and sacrifice in order to maintain the assigned time limit.
- Create a Google doc to document any editing changes made throughout rehearsals and send this final edit to me at the end of the project.
- This project will require scheduling significant rehearsal time outside of class and requires, at minimum, two full-cast rehearsals a week aside from the class time.
- At the end of each rehearsal week, your group's designated stage manager will send me a rehearsal log documenting hours and days of rehearsal as well as what was covered at each rehearsal.
- As an ensemble, you will be responsible for choosing a director within your group or choosing to group direct.
- You will create a sound design to support your interpretation of the play and also supply suggestions of costumes.
- In addition to the performance, each group will be responsible for providing a brief written analysis of the text editing process if additions and subtractions of text were made, how you developed the directorial concept for your one-hour play, and what challenges you encountered during the rehearsal process.

I will be both facilitating and observing your rehearsals. The project will be paneled by me, the head of the BFA Acting Program and a professor of voice and speech the week before finals week. Notes from the panel are to be incorporated during your final week of rehearsals. The process will culminate in a final presentation of the edited play (memorized) with an invited audience during finals week.

Editing exercise

Before beginning the One-Hour projects in a class setting, I always start with an editing exercise. It is a great jumping-off point for students and helps to demystify the challenges with editing Shakespearean text. The steps I follow are below:

- Step 1. Divide the class into four small groups and hand them all a copy of any two-person scene of your choice. I often choose the famous "nunnery" scene from *Hamlet* 3.1 starting with the "To be or not to be" speech and ending with Ophelia's famous monologue. This scene

is fairly short and self-contained and begins and ends with really well-known text that students have often already formed an opinion about.
- Step 2. Cast the groups. Assign one half of the actors as one character (Hamlet) and the other half as the second character (Ophelia). Assigning roles immediately gives students a more personal stake in either retaining or editing text and enforces a sense of ownership.
- Step 3. The students' in-class assignment, working together in their groups, is to cut the scene down by 50 percent of the lines. They have 20–25 minutes.
- Step 4. Observe the communications of each group and take note of the discussions, compromises and group text explorations. I will often write down quotes I hear each group make and read them back to the group, for example "This hurts," "But that is a famous line," "It is so repetitive – he has said this before," "But she has so little to say before this so let's not cut as much of her text," "I agree," etc. These observations can serve as talking points for a full class discussion following the exercise.
- Step 5. When the 20–25 minutes are up, and after reading student quotes, pick two members of each group to read through their newly edited version of the scene and then discuss why they chose to edit what they did, what it means to them, why they chose to keep in certain text and what were the main challenges.
- Step 6. After all groups have shared their edits then we discuss the similarities and differences within each group's edit. I encourage students to accept that there is not a "right" way to edit the plays.

4
CROSS-GENDER CASTING SUGGESTIONS

Cross-gender casting was a practice in Shakespearean times from the very first performances of his plays. In Shakespeare's time, *all* parts were played by men as women were not allowed on stage. Today, in casting plays, we have a choice. Shakespeare's plays lend themselves quite well to cross-gender casting whether in an educational environment or in professional productions. If you choose to have a female play a part originally written for a male, a male play a part designated as female, or a non-binary, transgender or gender-fluid actor play gender-specific roles, you have choices to consider with the text.

- Is the actor playing the part as written and not putting focus on gender? If so, my suggestion is to keep the text as is and not change the pronouns as written.
- Is the actor choosing to alter the gender of the character? If so, then my suggestion is to change the pronouns in the text to reflect that choice.

Here are some suggestions, a partial list, to consider of roles in this collection that have been successfully played as or by either gender.

> Jacques, Duke Senior, Silvius and Amiens in *As You Like It*
> Lafew in *All's Well That Ends Well*
> Cassius, Marc Antony and Casca in *Julius Caesar*
> Longaville and Boyet in *Love's Labour's Lost*

Escalus and Friar Thomas in *Measure for Measure*
Philostrate, Puck, Fairies and Mechanicals in *A Midsummer Night's Dream*
Mercutio, Prince, Benvolio and the Nurse in *Romeo and Juliet*
Othello, Iago and Roderigo in *Othello*
Hamlet, Horatio and Laertes in *Hamlet*
Antonio in *The Merchant of Venice*
Prospero, Caliban, Ariel and Stephano in *The Tempest*
Feste the clown in *Twelfth Night*
Polixenes in *The Winter's Tale*
Leonato, Don John, Don Pedro and Conrade in *Much Ado About Nothing*
Malcolm, Rosse and the Witches in *Macbeth*
Launce and Outlaws in *Two Gentlemen of Verona*

5
A MIDSUMMER NIGHT'S DREAM

William Shakespeare

Originally written – 1595–1596
First Published – 1600
First recorded performance – 1605

Edited and Abridged by Julie Fain Lawrence-Edsell
(adapted from http://shakespeare.mit.edu)

Dramatis Personae

THESEUS, Duke of Athens
HIPPOLYTA, Queen of the Amazons and betrothed of Theseus
EGEUS, father of Hermia
LYSANDER, beloved of Hermia
HERMIA, daughter to Egeus, in love with Lysander
HELENA, in love with Demetrius
DEMETRIUS, in love with Hermia but falls in love with Helena
PHILOSTRATE, Master of the Revels for Theseus

OBERON, King of Faries
PUCK, or Robin Goodfellow, servant to Oberon

TITANIA, Queen of Faries
PEASEBLOSSOM, fairy servant to Titania
COBWEB, fairy servant to Titania
MOTH, fairy servant to Titania
MUSTARDSEED, fairy servant to Titania

Other fairies attending on Oberon and Titania

PETER QUINCE, a carpenter that leads the troupe
NICK BOTTOM, a weaver who plays Pyramus
FRANCIS FLUTE, a bellows-mender who plays Thisbe
ROBIN STARVELING, plays Moonshine and is a tailor
TOM SNOUT, plays the wall and is a tinker
SNUG, plays the lion and is a joiner

ACT I, SCENE I. Athens. The palace of THESEUS.
Enter THESEUS, HIPPOLYTA, etc.

THESEUS
Now, fair Hippolyta, our nuptial hour
Draws on apace;[1] four happy days bring in
Another moon. –

HIPPOLYTA
Four days will quickly steep themselves in night;
Four nights will quickly dream away the time; 5
And then the moon, like to a silver bow
New-bent in heaven, shall behold the night
Of our solemnities.[2]

THESEUS
Hippolyta, I woo'd thee with my sword,
And won thy love, doing thee injuries;
But I will wed thee in another key, 10
With pomp, with triumph and with revelling.

Enter EGEUS, HERMIA, LYSANDER, and DEMETRIUS

EGEUS
Happy be Theseus, our renowned Duke!

THESEUS
Thanks, good Egeus: what's the news with thee?

EGEUS
Full of vexation[3] come I, with complaint
Against my child, my daughter Hermia. 15
Stand forth, Demetrius. My noble lord,
This man hath my consent to marry her.
Stand forth, Lysander: and my gracious Duke,
This man hath bewitch'd the bosom of my child.
Turn'd her obedience, which is due to me, 20
To stubborn harshness: and, my gracious Duke,

---
[1] apace – quickly
[2] solemnities – ceremonies performed, celebration of nuptials
[3] vexation – trouble, great uneasiness

Be it so she will not here before your Grace
Consent to marry with Demetrius,
I beg the ancient privilege of Athens:
As she is mine, I may dispose[4] of her;   25
Which shall be either to this gentleman
Or to her death, according to our law
Immediately provided in that case.

THESEUS
What say you, Hermia? Be advised fair maid.
Demetrius is a worthy gentleman.   30

HERMIA
So is Lysander.

THESEUS
             In himself he is;
But in this kind, wanting your father's voice,
The other must be held the worthier.

HERMIA
I would my father look'd but with my eyes.

THESEUS
Rather your eyes must with his judgement look.   35

HERMIA
I do entreat your Grace to pardon me;
I know not by what power I am made bold,
Nor how it may concern my modesty
In such a presence here to plead my thoughts,
But I beseech your Grace that I may know   40
The worst that may befall me in this case,
If I refuse to wed Demetrius.

THESEUS
Either to die the death or to abjure[5]
For ever the society of men.
Therefore, fair Hermia, question your desires;   45
Take time to pause; and, by the next new moon,

---

[4] dispose – to do with, bestow
[5] abjure – renounce upon oath

Upon that day either prepare to die
For disobedience to your father's will,
Or else to wed Demetrius, as he would.

DEMETRIUS
Relent, sweet Hermia; and, Lysander, yield   50
Thy crazed[6] title to my certain right.

LYSANDER
You have her father's love, Demetrius;
Let me have Hermia's; do you marry him.

EGEUS
Scornful Lysander!

LYSANDER
I am, my lord, as well derived[7] as he,   55
As well possess'd; my love is more than his;
I am beloved of beauteous Hermia.
Why should not I then prosecute my right?
Demetrius made love to Helena,
And won her soul; and she, sweet lady, dotes,[8] 60
Devoutly dotes, dotes in idolatry,
Upon this spotted[9] and inconstant man.

THESEUS
I must confess that I have heard so much;
But, Demetrius, come;
And come, Egeus; you shall go with me: 65
I have some private schooling for you both.
For you, fair Hermia, look you arm[10] yourself
To fit your fancies to your father's will;
Or else the law of Athens yields you up
To death, or to a vow of single life.   70

Exeunt all but LYSANDER and HERMIA

---

[6] crazed – invalid, flawed
[7] derived – descended, to be inherited
[8] dotes – love to excess, to be fond of
[9] spotted – guilty, polluted
[10] arm – prepare, provide

LYSANDER
Ay me!
The course of true love never did run smooth.

HERMIA
O hell! to choose love by another's eyes.

LYSANDER
Or, if there were a sympathy in choice,
War, death, or sickness did lay siege to it: 75
The jaws of darkness do devour it up:
So quick bright things come to confusion.

HERMIA
If then true lovers have been ever cross'd,
It stands as an edict[11] in destiny.
Then let us teach our trial patience, 80
Wishes and tears, poor fancy's[12] followers.

LYSANDER
A good persuasion: therefore, hear me, Hermia.
I have a widow aunt, a dowager
Of great revenue, and she hath no child:
From Athens is her house remote seven leagues; 85
And she respects me as her only son.
There, gentle Hermia, may I marry thee,
And to that place the sharp[13] Athenian law
Cannot pursue us.

HERMIA
　　　　　　My good Lysander!
I swear to thee, by Cupid's strongest bow,
Tomorrow truly will I meet with thee. 90

LYSANDER
Keep promise, love. Look, here comes Helena.

Enter HELENA

---

[11] edict – decree, law
[12] fancy – liking, taste
[13] sharp – harsh, severe

HERMIA
God speed fair Helena! Whither away?

HELENA
Call you me fair? That fair again unsay.
Demetrius loves your fair: O happy fair!   95
Yours would I catch,[14] fair Hermia, ere I go:
Were the world mine, Demetrius being bated,[15]
The rest I'd give to be to you translated.
O, teach me how you look, and with what art
You sway the motion[16] of Demetrius' heart.   100

HERMIA
I frown upon him, yet he loves me still.

HELENA
O that your frowns would teach my smiles such skill!

HERMIA
The more I hate, the more he follows me.

HELENA
The more I love, the more he hateth me.

HERMIA
His folly,[17] Helena, is no fault of mine.   105

HELENA
None, but your beauty: would that fault were mine!

HERMIA
Take comfort: he no more shall see my face;
Lysander and myself will fly this place.

LYSANDER
Helen, to you our minds we will unfold:
Tomorrow night,   110
Through Athens' gates have we devised to steal.[18]

---

[14] catch – to receive by contagion or affection
[15] bated – remitted, excepted
[16] motion – movement of soul, impulse
[17] folly – excessive desire
[18] steal – to come or go secretly

HERMIA
Farewell, sweet playfellow; pray thou for us,
And good luck grant thee thy Demetrius!
Keep word, Lysander; we must starve our sight
From lovers' food till morrow deep midnight. 115

LYSANDER
I will, my Hermia.

Exit HERMIA

          Helena, adieu:
As you on him, Demetrius dote on you!

Exit

HELENA
How happy some o'er other some can be!
Through Athens I am thought as fair as she.
But what of that? Demetrius thinks not so; 120
He will not know what all but he do know:
And as he errs,[19] doting on Hermia's eyes,
So I, admiring of his qualities:
Things base and vile, holding no quantity,
Love can transpose to form and dignity: 125
Love looks not with the eyes, but with the mind;
And therefore is wing'd Cupid painted blind.
Nor hath Love's mind of any judgement taste;
Wings and no eyes figure unheedy haste:
As waggish[20] boys in game themselves forswear, 130
So the boy Love is perjured everywhere:
For ere Demetrius look'd on Hermia's eyne,[21]
He hail'd down oaths that he was only mine;
And when this hail some heat from Hermia felt,
So he dissolv'd,[22] and showers of oaths did melt. 135
I will go tell him of fair Hermia's flight:

---

[19] errs – stray, deviate from the true course
[20] waggish – wanton, frolicsome, promiscuous
[21] eyne – eyes
[22] dissolv'd – melted

Then to the wood will he, tomorrow night,
Pursue her; and for this intelligence
If I have thanks, it is a dear[23] expense.
But herein mean I to enrich my pain,   140
To have his sight thither and back again.

Exit

ACT I, SCENE II. Athens. QUINCE's house.
Enter QUINCE, SNUG, BOTTOM, FLUTE, SNOUT, and STARVELING

QUINCE
Is all our company here?

BOTTOM
You were best to call them generally, man by man, according to the scrip.[24]

QUINCE
Here is the scroll of every man's name, which is thought fit, through all Athens, to play in our interlude[25] before the Duke and the Duchess, on his wedding-day at night.   5

BOTTOM
First, good Peter Quince, say what the play treats on,[26] then read the names of the actors, and so grow to a point.

QUINCE
Marry, our play is, 'The most lamentable comedy, and most cruel death of Pyramus and Thisbe'.   10

BOTTOM
Now, good Peter Quince, call forth your actors by the scroll.

QUINCE
Answer as I call you. Nick Bottom, the weaver.

BOTTOM
Ready. Name what part I am for, and proceed.

---
[23] dear – expensive
[24] scrip – script
[25] interlude – play performed in the intervals of a festivity
[26] treats on – speaks about, has for a subject

QUINCE
You, Nick Bottom, are set down for Pyramus.

BOTTOM
What is Pyramus? A lover, or a tyrant? 15

QUINCE
A lover, that kills himself most gallant for love.

BOTTOM
That will ask some tears in the true performing of it: if I do it, let the audience look to their eyes; I will move storms. Now name the rest of the players.

QUINCE
Francis Flute, the bellows-mender.[27] 20

FLUTE
Here, Peter Quince.

QUINCE
Flute, you must take Thisbe on you.

FLUTE
What is Thisbe? A wandering knight?

QUINCE
It is the lady that Pyramus must love.

FLUTE
Nay, faith, let me not play a woman; I have a beard coming. 25

QUINCE
That's all one: you shall play it in a mask, and you may speak as small as you will.

BOTTOM
And I may hide my face, let me play Thisbe too. I'll speak in a monstrous little voice. 'Thisne'; 'Ah, Pyramus, my lover dear!'

QUINCE
No, no; you must play Pyramus; and, Flute, you Thisbe. 30

---

[27] bellows-mender – fixer of the instrument used to blow a fire

BOTTOM
Well, proceed.

QUINCE
Robin Starveling, the tailor.

STARVELING
Here, Peter Quince.

QUINCE
Robin Starveling, you must play Thisbe's mother. Tom Snout, the tinker.[28]   35

SNOUT
Here, Peter Quince.

QUINCE
You, Pyramus' father; myself, Thisbe's father; Snug, the joiner;[29] you, the lion's part: and, I hope, here is a play fitted.

SNUG
Have you the lion's part written? Pray you, if it be, give it me, for I am slow of study.   40

QUINCE
You may do it extempore,[30] for it is nothing but roaring.

BOTTOM
Let me play the lion too. I will roar, that I will make the Duke say 'Let him roar again, let him roar again!'

QUINCE
And you should do it too terribly, you would fright the Duchess and the ladies, that they would shriek; and that were   45 enough to hang us all.

ALL
That would hang us, every mother's son.

BOTTOM
I grant you I will roar you as gently as any sucking dove.[31]

---

[28] tinker – mender of old brass
[29] joiner – maker of wooden furniture
[30] extempore – done without preparation
[31] sucking dove – to draw in, to be at the breast

QUINCE
You can play no part but Pyramus.

BOTTOM
Well, I will undertake it. 50

QUINCE
Masters, here are your parts: con[32] them by tomorrow night; and meet me in the palace wood, a mile without the town, by moonlight; there will we rehearse. I pray you, fail me not.

BOTTOM
We will meet; and there we may rehearse most obscenely and courageously. Take pains, be perfect: adieu. 55

QUINCE
At the Duke's oak we meet.

BOTTOM
Enough; hold or cut bow-strings.[33]

Exeunt

ACT II, SCENE I. A wood near Athens.
Enter a Fairy, and PUCK

PUCK
How now, spirit! Whither wander you?

Fairy
Over hill, over dale,[34]
Thorough[35] bush, thorough brier,[36]
Over park, over pale,
Thorough flood, thorough fire, 5
I do wander everywhere,
Swifter than the moon's sphere;

---

[32] con — learn by heart
[33] cut bow-strings — "come what come may"
[34] dale — valley
[35] thorough — through
[36] brier — wild species of the rose

And I serve the Fairy Queen.
Farewell, thou lob[37] of spirits; I'll be gone:
Our Queen and all our elves come here anon.   10

PUCK
The King doth keep his revels here tonight:
Take heed the Queen come not within his sight;
Because that she as her attendant hath
A lovely boy, stolen from an Indian king;
She never had so sweet a changeling;[38]   15
And jealous Oberon would have the child.
But she perforce withholds the loved boy,
And, they do square,[39] that all their elves for fear
Creep into acorn-cups and hide them there.

Fairy
Either I mistake your shape and making quite,   20
Or else you are that shrewd and knavish sprite
Call'd Robin Goodfellow. Are not you he?

PUCK
Thou speak'st aright;
I am that merry wanderer of the night.
I jest[40] to Oberon and make him smile.   25
And sometime lurk I in a gossip's[41] bowl
In very likeness of a roasted crab,[42]
And when she drinks, against her lips bob
And on her withered dewlap[43] pour the ale.
A merrier hour was never wasted there,   30
But room, fairy! Here comes Oberon.

Fairy
And here my mistress. Would that he were gone!

---

[37] lob – lout, term of contempt
[38] changeling – a child left or taken by the fairies
[39] square – quarrel
[40] jest – to play, to joke
[41] gossip's – tattling woman
[42] crab – wild apple
[43] dewlap – hanging breast

Enter, from one side, OBERON, with his train; from the other, TITANIA, with hers

OBERON
Ill met by moonlight, proud Titania.

TITANIA
What, jealous Oberon? Fairies, skip hence;
I have forsworn his bed and company.   35

OBERON
Tarry, rash wanton;[44] am not I thy lord?

TITANIA
Then I must be thy lady – Why art thou here,
But that, forsooth, the bouncing Amazon,
Your buskin'd[45] mistress and your warrior love,
To Theseus must be wedded, and you come   40
To give their bed joy and prosperity?

OBERON
How canst thou thus, for shame, Titania,
Glance[46] at my credit with Hippolyta,
Knowing I know thy love to Theseus?

TITANIA
These are the forgeries[47] of jealousy: 45
And never, since the middle summer's spring,
Met we on hill, in dale, forest or mead,[48]
By paved fountain or by rushy brook,
Or in the beached margent[49] of the sea,
To dance our ringlets[50] to the whistling wind,   50
But with thy brawls thou hast disturb'd our sport.
Therefore the winds, piping to us in vain,
As in revenge, have suck'd up from the sea
Contagious fogs; which, falling in the land

---

[44] wanton – lascivious woman
[45] buskin'd – dressed in knee-high boots
[46] glance – hint
[47] forgeries – deceptions, lies
[48] mead – flat and low grass-covered land
[49] beached margent – flat strand, margin or border
[50] ringlets – small circles

Have every pelting[51] river made so proud 55
That they have overborne their continents:
Therefore the moon, the governess of floods,
Pale in her anger, washes all the air,
That rheumatic diseases do abound.
The seasons alter: the spring, the summer, 60
The childing[52] autumn, angry winter, change
Their wonted liveries,[53] and the mazed world,
By their increase, now knows not which is which.
And this same progeny of evils comes
From our debate, from our dissension; 65
We are their parents and original.[54]

OBERON
Do you amend it then; it lies in you.
Why should Titania cross her Oberon?
I do but beg a little changeling boy,
To be my henchman.

TITANIA
                Set your heart at rest: 70
The fairy land buys not the child of me.
His mother was a votaress[55] of my order:
But she, being mortal, of that boy did die;
And for her sake do I rear up her boy,
And for her sake I will not part with him. 75

OBERON
How long within this wood intend you stay?

TITANIA
Perchance till after Theseus' wedding-day.
If you will patiently dance in our round
And see our moonlight revels, go with us;
If not, shun[56] me, and I will spare your haunts.[57] 80

---

[51] pelting – small, meager
[52] childing – fruitful
[53] wonted liveries – customary appearances
[54] original – origin
[55] votaress – a woman that has taken a vow to serve and follow
[56] shun – avoid, try to escape
[57] haunts – a place visited often

OBERON
Give me that boy, and I will go with thee.

TITANIA
Not for thy fairy kingdom. Fairies, away!
We shall chide downright, if I longer stay.

Exit TITANIA with her train

OBERON
Well, go thy way: thou shalt not from this grove
Till I torment thee for this injury.[58]   85
My gentle Puck, come hither. Thou rememberest
Since once I sat upon a promontory,[59]
To hear a mermaid's music –

PUCK
                    I remember.

OBERON
That very time I saw, but thou couldst not,
Cupid all arm'd; a certain aim he took   90
As it should pierce a hundred thousand hearts.
Well mark'd I where the bolt of Cupid fell:
It fell upon a little western flower,
Before milk-white, now purple with love's wound,
And maidens call it 'love-in-idleness'.   95
Fetch me that flower; the herb I show'd thee once:
The juice of it on sleeping eye-lids laid
Will make or man or woman madly dote
Upon the next live creature that it sees.

PUCK
I'll put a girdle[60] round about the earth   100
In forty minutes.

Exit

---

[58] injury – offence, insult
[59] promontory – high headland, cape, peninsula
[60] girdle – belt around the waist, enclosed circle

OBERON
                Having once this juice,
I'll watch Titania when she is asleep,
And drop the liquor of it in her eyes.
The next thing then she waking looks upon,
Be it on lion, bear, or wolf, or bull,   105
On meddling monkey, or on busy ape,
She shall pursue it with the soul of love.
But who comes here? I am invisible;
And I will overhear their conference.

Enter DEMETRIUS, HELENA, following him

DEMETRIUS
I love thee not, therefore pursue me not.   110
Where is Lysander and fair Hermia?
The one I'll slay, the other slayeth me.
Hence, get thee gone, and follow me no more.

HELENA
You draw me, you hard-hearted adamant;[61]
But yet you draw not iron, for my heart   115
Is true as steel. Leave you your power to draw,
And I shall have no power to follow you.

DEMETRIUS
Do I entice you? Do I speak you fair?
Or, rather, do I not in plainest truth
Tell you, I do not, nor I cannot love you?   120

HELENA
And even for that do I love you the more.
I am your spaniel; and, Demetrius,
The more you beat me, I will fawn on you.
What worser place can I beg in your love, –
Than to be used as you use your dog?   125

DEMETRIUS
Tempt not too much the hatred of my spirit;
For I am sick when I do look on thee.

---

[61] adamant – magnet, thing of focus or attraction

HELENA
And I am sick when I look not on you.

DEMETRIUS
I'll run from thee and hide me in the brakes,[62]
And leave thee to the mercy of wild beasts. 130

HELENA
The wildest hath not such a heart as you.

DEMETRIUS
I will not stay thy questions; let me go:
Or, if thou follow me, do not believe
But I shall do thee mischief[63] in the wood.

HELENA
You do me mischief. Fie, Demetrius! 135
Your wrongs do set a scandal on my sex.
We cannot fight for love, as men may do;
We should be woo'd and were not made to woo.

Exit DEMETRIUS

I'll follow thee and make a heaven of hell,
To die upon the hand I love so well. 140

Exit

OBERON
Fare thee well, nymph: ere[64] he do leave this grove,
Thou shalt fly[65] him, and he shall seek thy love.

Re-enter PUCK

Hast thou the flower there?

PUCK
Ay, there it is.

---
[62] brakes – thickets
[63] mischief – harm, injury, evil done on purpose
[64] ere – before
[65] fly – flee

OBERON
                    I pray thee, give it me.
I know a bank where the wild thyme blows,   145
There sleeps Titania sometime of the night;
And with the juice of this I'll streak[66] her eyes,
And make her full of hateful[67] fantasies.
Take thou some of it, and seek through this grove:
A sweet Athenian lady is in love   150
With a disdainful youth: anoint[68] his eyes;
But do it when the next thing he espies[69]
May be the lady: thou shalt know the man
By the Athenian garments he hath on.

PUCK
Fear not, my lord, your servant shall do so.   155

Exeunt

ACT II, SCENE II. Another part of the wood.
Enter TITANIA, with her train

TITANIA
Come, now a roundel[70] and a fairy song;
Sing me now asleep;
Then to your offices and let me rest.

Fairies
(Singing) You spotted snakes with double tongue,
Thorny hedgehogs, be not seen;   5
Newts[71] and blind-worms, do no wrong,
Come not near our fairy queen.
Philomel, with melody
Sing in our sweet lullaby;
Lulla, lulla, lullaby, lulla, lulla, lullaby: 10
Never harm, nor spell, nor charm,
Come our lovely lady nigh;[72]

---

[66] streak – spread over with a liquid substance
[67] hateful – disgusting, ugly
[68] anoint – spread over with a liquid substance
[69] espies – discover, to see
[70] roundel – dance in a circle
[71] newts – small lizards
[72] nigh – near

So, good night, with lullaby.
Philomel, with melody
Sing in our sweet lullaby; 15
Lulla, lulla, lullaby, lulla, lulla, lullaby.

TITANIA sleeps

Fairy
Hence, away! now all is well.

Exeunt Fairies
Enter OBERON and squeezes the flower on TITANIA's eyelids

OBERON
What thou seest when thou dost wake,
Do it for thy true-love take;
Be it ounce,[73] or cat, or bear, 20
When thou wakest, it is thy dear.
Wake when some vile thing is near.

Exit
Enter LYSANDER and HERMIA

LYSANDER
Fair love, you faint with wandering in the wood,
And to speak troth, I have forgot our way.
We'll rest us, Hermia, if you think it good, 25
And tarry[74] for the comfort of the day.

HERMIA
Be it so, Lysander: find you out a bed;
For I upon this bank will rest my head.

LYSANDER
One turf shall serve as pillow for us both;
One heart, one bed, two bosoms and one troth. 30

HERMIA
Nay, good Lysander; for my sake, my dear,
Lie further off yet, do not lie so near.

---
[73] ounce – snow leopard
[74] tarry – stay, wait

LYSANDER
O, take the sense, sweet, of my innocence!
Love takes the meaning in love's conference.
Two bosoms interchained[75] with an oath;   35
So then two bosoms and a single troth.[76]
Then by your side no bed-room me deny;
For lying so, Hermia, I do not lie.

HERMIA
Lysander riddles very prettily:
Now much beshrew my manners and my pride,   40
If Hermia meant to say Lysander lied.
But, gentle friend, for love and courtesy,
Lie further off, in human modesty;
Such separation as may well be said
Becomes a virtuous bachelor and a maid,   45
So far be distant; and, good night, sweet friend:
Thy love ne'er alter till thy sweet life end!

LYSANDER
Here is my bed: sleep give thee all his rest!

They sleep
Enter PUCK

PUCK
Through the forest have I gone.
But Athenian found I none,   50
Night and silence – Who is here?
Weeds of Athens he doth wear:
This is he, my master said,
Despised the Athenian maid;
And here the maiden, sleeping sound,   55
On the dank[77] and dirty ground.
Churl,[78] upon thy eyes I throw
All the power this charm doth owe.
So awake when I am gone;

---

[75] interchained – linked together
[76] troth – truth
[77] dank – damp
[78] churl – rude and ill-bred fellow

For I must now to Oberon. 60

Exit PUCK
Enter DEMETRIUS and HELENA, running

HELENA
Stay, though thou kill me, sweet Demetrius.

DEMETRIUS
I charge thee, hence, and do not haunt me thus.
Stay, on thy peril: I alone will go.

Exit

HELENA
O, I am out of breath in this fond chase!
The more my prayer, the lesser is my grace. 65
Happy is Hermia, wheresoe'er she lies,
For she hath blessed and attractive eyes.
How came her eyes so bright? Not with salt tears:
If so, my eyes are oftener wash'd than hers.
No, no, I am as ugly as a bear, 70
For beasts that meet me run away for fear:
Therefore no marvel though Demetrius
Do, as a monster, fly[79] my presence thus.
What wicked and dissembling glass[80] of mine
Made me compare with Hermia's sphery[81] eyne? 75
But who is here? Lysander, on the ground!
Dead, or asleep? I see no blood, no wound.
Lysander if you live, good sir, awake.

LYSANDER
(*Waking*) And run through fire I will for thy sweet sake!
Transparent Helena! Nature shows art, 80
That through thy bosom makes me see thy heart.
Where is Demetrius? O, how fit a word
Is that vile name to perish on my sword!

---

[79] fly – flee
[80] dissembling glass – mirror that gives a false appearance
[81] sphery – star-like, celestial

HELENA
Do not say so, Lysander; say not so
What though he love your Hermia? Lord, what though? 85
Yet Hermia still loves you; then be content.

LYSANDER
Content with Hermia! No; I do repent
The tedious minutes I with her have spent.
Not Hermia but Helena I love:
Who will not change a raven for a dove? 90

HELENA
Wherefore was I to this keen[82] mockery born?
When at your hands did I deserve this scorn?
Is't not enough, is't not enough, young man,
That I did never, no, nor never can,
Deserve a sweet look from Demetrius' eye, 95
But you must flout[83] my insufficiency?
Good troth, you do me wrong, good sooth, you do,
In such disdainful manner me to woo.
O, that a lady, of one man refused,
Should of another therefore be abused! 100

Exit HELENA

LYSANDER
She sees not Hermia. Hermia, sleep thou there:
And never mayst thou come Lysander near!
So thou, my surfeit[84] and my heresy,[85]
Of all be hated, but the most of me!
And, all my powers, address your love and might 105
To honour Helen and to be her knight!

Exit LYSANDER

HERMIA
(*Waking*) Help me, Lysander, help me! Do thy best
To pluck this crawling serpent from my breast!

---

[82] keen – bitter, sarcastic
[83] flout – to mock, to make a fool of
[84] surfeit – sickness and feeling full caused by gluttony
[85] heresy – opinion differing from the established faith

Lysander! what, removed? Lysander! Lord!
Alack, where are you? Speak, an if you hear; 110
No? Then I well perceive you are not nigh[86]
Either death or you I'll find immediately.

Exit

ACT III, SCENE I. The wood. TITANIA lying asleep.
Enter QUINCE, SNUG, BOTTOM, FLUTE, SNOUT, and STARVELING

BOTTOM
Are we all met?

QUINCE
Pat, pat; and here's a marvellous convenient place for our rehearsal.

BOTTOM
Peter Quince, –

QUINCE
What sayest thou, bully Bottom?

BOTTOM
There are things in this comedy of Pyramus and Thisbe that will 5
never please. First, Pyramus must draw a sword to kill himself;
which the ladies cannot abide.[87] How answer you that?

SNOUT
By'rlakin,[88] a parlous[89] fear.

STARVELING
I believe we must leave the killing out, when all is done.

BOTTOM
Write me a prologue, and let the prologue seem to say we will 10
do no harm with our swords, and that Pyramus is not killed
indeed. This will put them out of fear.

QUINCE
Well, we will have such a prologue.

---
[86] nigh – near
[87] abide – endure
[88] By'rlakin – a mild oath, byrlady, by our lady-kin
[89] parlous – perilous, alarming

SNOUT
Will not the ladies be afeard of the lion?

STARVELING
I fear it, I promise you.

BOTTOM
God shield us! A lion among ladies, is a most dreadful thing;
for there is not a more fearful wild-fowl[90] than your lion living.

SNOUT
Therefore another prologue must tell he is not a lion.

BOTTOM
Nay, you must name his name, and half his face must be seen through
the lion's neck: and he himself must speak through, saying thus
'If you think I come hither as a lion, it were pity of my life: no,
I am no such thing; I am a man as other men are': and there let
him name his name, and tell them plainly he is Snug the joiner.

QUINCE
Well it shall be so. But there is two hard things; that is, to bring
the moonlight into a chamber; for, you know, Pyramus and Thisbe
meet by moonlight.

SNOUT
Doth the moon shine that night we play our play?

QUINCE
Yes, it doth shine that night.

BOTTOM
Why, then may you leave a casement of the great chamber
window open and the moon may shine in at the casement.

QUINCE
Ay; or else one must come in and say he comes to present[91]
the person of Moonshine. Then, there is another thing: we
must have a wall in the great chamber; for Pyramus and Thisbe,
says the story, did talk through the chink[92] of a wall.

---

[90] wild-fowl – undomesticated birds
[91] present – act, perform
[92] chink – fissure, narrow opening, crack

SNOUT
You can never bring in a wall. What say you, Bottom? 35

BOTTOM
Some man or other must present Wall: and let him hold his fingers thus, and through that cranny[93] shall Pyramus and Thisbe whisper.

QUINCE
If that may be, then all is well. Come, sit down, every mother's son, and rehearse your parts. Pyramus, you begin: and so every one according to his cue. 40

Enter PUCK behind

PUCK
What hempen home-spuns[94] have we swaggering here,
So near the cradle of the Fairy Queen?
What, a play toward![95] I'll be an auditor;
An actor too, perhaps, if I see cause.

Exit

QUINCE
Speak, Pyramus. Thisbe, stand forth. 45

BOTTOM
Thisbe, the flowers of odious[96] savours sweet, –

QUINCE
'Odours'! 'odours'!

BOTTOM
Odours savours sweet:
So hath thy breath, my dearest Thisbe dear.
But hark, a voice! Stay thou but here awhile,
And by and by I will to thee appear. 50

---

[93] cranny – fissure, narrow opening, crack
[94] hempen home-spuns – ill-mannered and coarse person
[95] toward – in preparation and expectation, near at hand
[96] odious – hateful

PUCK
A stranger Pyramus than e'er played here.

Exit PUCK

FLUTE
Must I speak now?

QUINCE
Ay, marry, must you.

FLUTE
Most radiant Pyramus, most lily-white of hue,
As true as truest horse that yet would never tire. 55
I'll meet thee, Pyramus, at Ninny's tomb.

QUINCE
'Ninus' tomb', man! Why, you must not speak that yet. That you answer to Pyramus. You speak all your part at once, cues and all. Pyramus, enter. Your cue is past. It is 'never tire'.

Re-enter PUCK, and BOTTOM with an ass's head on

BOTTOM
If I were fair, Thisbe, I were only thine. 60

QUINCE
O monstrous! O strange! We are haunted. Pray, masters! fly, masters! Help!

Exeunt QUINCE, SNUG, FLUTE, SNOUT, and STARVELING

PUCK
I'll follow you, I'll lead you about a round,
Through bog, through bush, through brake,[97] through brier.
Sometime a horse I'll be, sometime a hound, 65
And neigh, and bark, and grunt, and roar, and burn.

Exit PUCK

---

[97] brake – thicket

BOTTOM
Why do they run away? This is a knavery of them to make me afeard.

Enter all

QUINCE
Bless thee, Bottom, bless thee! thou art translated.[98]

Exeunt all, except BOTTOM

BOTTOM
I see their knavery: this is to make an ass of me; to fright me, if they could. But I will not stir from this place, do what they can: I will walk up and down here, and I will sing, that they shall hear I am not afraid.
(*Sings*)
The ousel[99] cock so black of hue,
With orange-tawny bill,
The throstle[100] with his note so true,
The wren with little quill,[101] –

70

75

TITANIA
(*Awaking*) What angel wakes me from my flowery bed?
I pray thee, gentle mortal, sing again:
Mine ear is much enamour'd of thy note;
So is mine eye enthralled to thy shape;
And thy fair virtue's force perforce[102] doth move me
On the first view to say, to swear, I love thee.

80

BOTTOM
Methinks, mistress, you should have little reason for that: and yet, to say the truth, reason and love keep little company together nowadays.

85

TITANIA
Thou art as wise as thou art beautiful.

---

[98] translated – transformed, changed
[99] ousel – blackbird
[100] throstle – song bird with a loud and repetitive song
[101] quill – feather pen
[102] force perforce – at any rate, in the same sense

BOTTOM
Not so, neither; but if I had wit enough to get out of this wood,
I have enough to serve mine own turn.

TITANIA
Out of this wood do not desire to go: 90
Thou shalt remain here, whether thou wilt or no.
I am a spirit of no common rate;
The summer still doth tend upon my state;
And I do love thee: therefore, go with me;
I'll give thee fairies to attend on thee, 95
And they shall fetch thee jewels from the deep,
And sing while thou on pressed flowers dost sleep;
Peaseblossom! Cobweb! Moth! and Mustardseed!

Enter PEASEBLOSSOM, COBWEB, MOTH, and MUSTARDSEED

PEASEBLOSSOM
Ready.

COBWEB
    And I.

MOTH
        And I.

MUSTARDSEED
        And I.

ALL
            Where shall we go?

TITANIA
Be kind and courteous to this gentleman; 100
Nod to him, elves, and do him courtesies.

PEASEBLOSSOM
Hail, mortal!

COBWEB
    Hail!

MOTH
        Hail!

MUSTARDSEED
                    Hail!

TITANIA
Come, wait upon him; lead him to my bower.[103]
Tie up my love's tongue bring him silently.

Exeunt

ACT III, SCENE II. Another part of the wood.
Enter OBERON

OBERON
I wonder if Titania be awaked;
Then, what it was that next came in her eye,
Which she must dote on in extremity.

Enter PUCK

PUCK
My mistress with a monster is in love.
While she was in her dull and sleeping hour,   5
A crew of patches,[104] rude mechanicals,
Were met together to rehearse a play
Intended for great Theseus' nuptial-day.
The shallowest thick-skin of that barren sort,   10
Who Pyramus presented, in their sport
Forsook his scene and enter'd in a brake,
When I did him at this advantage take:
An ass's nole[105] I fixed on his head.
Anon his Thisbe must be answered,   15
And forth my mimic comes. When they him spy –
So, at his sight, away his fellows fly.
When in that moment, so it came to pass,
Titania waked and straightway loved an ass.

---

[103] bower – arbor, shady recess among trees and flowers
[104] patches – paltry and beggarly fellows
[105] nole – head

OBERON
This falls out better than I could devise. 20
But hast thou yet latch'd[106] the Athenian's eyes
With the love-juice, as I did bid thee do?

PUCK
I took him sleeping – that is finish'd too –

Enter HERMIA and DEMETRIUS

OBERON
Stand close: this is the same Athenian.

PUCK
This is the woman, but not this the man. 25

DEMETRIUS
O, why rebuke you him that loves you so?

HERMIA
If thou hast slain Lysander in his sleep,
Being o'er[107] shoes in blood, plunge in the deep,
And kill me too.
The sun was not so true unto the day 30
As he to me. Would he have stolen away
From sleeping Hermia? Where is he?
Ah, good Demetrius, wilt thou give him me?

DEMETRIUS
I had rather give his carcass to my hounds.

HERMIA
Out, dog! out, cur! thou drivest me past the bounds 35
Of maiden's patience. Hast thou slain him, then?

DEMETRIUS
I am not guilty of Lysander's blood;
Nor is he dead, for aught that I can tell.

HERMIA
I pray thee, tell me then that he is well.

---

[106] latch'd – smeared over, caught
[107] o'er – passing beyond

DEMETRIUS
An if I could, what should I get therefore? 40

HERMIA
A privilege never to see me more.
And from thy hated presence part I so.

Exit HERMIA

DEMETRIUS
There is no following her in this fierce vein;
Here therefore for a while I will remain.

Lies down and sleeps

OBERON
What hast thou done? Thou hast mistaken quite 45
And laid the love-juice on some true-love's sight:
About the wood go swifter than the wind,
And Helena of Athens look thou find:
By some illusion see thou bring her here:
I'll charm his eyes against[108] she do appear. 50

PUCK
I go, I go; look how I go!

Exit

OBERON
(*Squeezing juice on Demetrius's eyelids*)
Flower of this purple dye,
Hit with Cupid's archery,
When thou wakest, if she be by,
Beg of her for remedy. 55

Re-enter PUCK

PUCK
Captain of our fairy band,
Helena is here at hand;

---

[108] against – in expectation of, for the time when

And the youth, mistook by me,
Pleading for a lover's fee.
Shall we their fond pageant see? 60
Lord, what fools these mortals be!

OBERON
Stand aside: the noise they make
Will cause Demetrius to awake.

Enter LYSANDER and HELENA

LYSANDER
Why should you think that I should woo in scorn?
Scorn and derision[109] never come in tears. 65
How can these things in me seem scorn to you,
Bearing the badge of faith, to prove them true?

HELENA
You do advance your cunning more and more.
When truth kills truth, O devilish-holy fray!
These vows are Hermia's: will you give her o'er? 70

LYSANDER
I had no judgement when to her I swore.

HELENA
Nor none, in my mind, now you give her o'er.

LYSANDER
Demetrius loves her, and he loves not you.

DEMETRIUS
(*Awaking*) O Helen, goddess, nymph, perfect, divine!
To what, my love, shall I compare thine eyne? 75
When thou hold'st up thy hand: O, let me kiss
This princess of pure white, this seal of bliss!

HELENA
O spite! O hell! I see you all are bent
To set against me for your merriment.
Can you not hate me, as I know you do, 80
But you must join in souls to mock me too?

---

[109] derision – laughing in contempt, scorn

If you were men, as men you are in show,
You would not use a gentle lady so.
You both are rivals, and love Hermia;
And now both rivals, to mock Helena. 85
A trim exploit, a manly enterprise,
To conjure tears up in a poor maid's eyes
With your derision! None of noble sort
Would so offend a virgin, and extort[110]
A poor soul's patience, all to make you sport. 90

LYSANDER
You are unkind, Demetrius; be not so;
For you love Hermia; this you know I know:
And here, with all good will, with all my heart,
In Hermia's love I yield you up my part;
And yours of Helena to me bequeath, 95
Whom I do love and will do till my death.

HELENA
Never did mockers waste more idle[111] breath.

DEMETRIUS
Lysander, keep thy Hermia; I will none.
If e'er I loved her, all that love is gone.
My heart to her but as guest-wise sojourn'd,[112] 100
And now to Helen is it home return'd.
Look, where thy love comes; yonder is thy dear.

Re-enter HERMIA

HERMIA
Thou art not by mine eye, Lysander, found;
Mine ear, I thank it, brought me to thy sound.
But why unkindly didst thou leave me so? 105

LYSANDER
Why should he stay, whom love doth press to go?

HERMIA
What love could press Lysander from my side?

---

[110] extort – draw by force, make impatient
[111] idle – useless, futile
[112] guest-wise sojourn'd – to dwell for a time like a stranger

LYSANDER
Fair Helena, who more engilds[113] the night
Than all you fiery oes and eyes[114] of light.
Why seek'st thou me? Could not this make thee know,   110
The hate I bear thee made me leave thee so?

HERMIA
You speak not as you think: it cannot be.

HELENA
Lo, she is one of this confederacy![115]
Now I perceive they have conjoin'd all three
To fashion[116] this false sport, in spite of me.   115
Injurious Hermia! Most ungrateful maid!
Have you conspired, have you with these contrived
To bait me with this foul derision?
Is all the counsel that we two have shared,
The sisters' vows, the hours that we have spent,   120
When we have chid the hasty-footed time
For parting us, – O, is it all forgot?
We, Hermia, like two artificial gods,
Have with our needles created both one flower,
As if our hands, our sides, voices, and minds,   125
Had been incorporate.[117] So we grew together,
Like to a double cherry on one stem;
And will you rent[118] our ancient love asunder,
To join with men in scorning your poor friend?

HERMIA
I am amazed at your passionate words.   130
I scorn you not: it seems that you scorn me.

HELENA
Have you not set Lysander, as in scorn,
To follow me and praise my eyes and face?
And made your other love, Demetrius,

---

[113] engilds – to make brilliant, to gild
[114] oes and eyes – orbs and stars
[115] confederacy – conspiracy, alliance
[116] fashion – contrive, bring about
[117] incorporate – made one body
[118] rent – split, tear

Who even but now did spurn me with his foot, 135
To call me goddess, nymph, divine, and rare,
Precious, celestial? Wherefore speaks he this
To her he hates? And wherefore doth Lysander
Deny your love, so rich within his soul,
And tender[119] me, forsooth, affection, 140
But by your setting on, by your consent?

HERMIA
I understand not what you mean by this.

HELENA
If you have any pity, grace, or manners,
You would not make me such an argument.
But fare ye well: 'tis partly my own fault, 145
Which death or absence soon shall remedy.

LYSANDER
Stay, gentle Helena; hear my excuse:
My love, my life, my soul, fair Helena!

HELENA
O excellent!

HERMIA
    Sweet, do not scorn her so.

LYSANDER
Helen, I love thee; by my life, I do. 150

DEMETRIUS
I say I love thee more than he can do.

LYSANDER
If thou say so, withdraw, and prove it too.

DEMETRIUS
Quick, come!

HERMIA
    Lysander, whereto tends[120] all this?

---

[119] tender – a thing offered
[120] tends – to move in a certain direction

LYSANDER
Hang off, thou cat, thou burr! Vile thing, let loose!

HERMIA
Why are you grown so rude? What change is this?   155

LYSANDER
Out, tawny Tartar,[121] out!

HERMIA
                    Do you not jest?

LYSANDER
Be certain, nothing truer; 'tis no jest
That I do hate thee and love Helena.

HERMIA
O me! (*To HELENA*) You juggler! You canker-blossom![122]
You thief of love! What, have you come by night   160
And stolen my love's heart from him?

HELENA
Fie, fie! You counterfeit![123] You puppet, you!

HERMIA
'Puppet'? Why so? Ay, that way goes the game.
Because I am so dwarfish and so low?
How low am I, thou painted maypole? Speak;   165
How low am I? I am not yet so low
But that my nails can reach unto thine eyes.

HELENA
Let her not strike me. You perhaps may think,
Because she is something lower than myself,
That I can match her.

HERMIA
                    'Lower'! Hark, again!   170

---

[121] tawny tartar – native of Tartary (ancient Northern Asia) with a yellowish-dark color
[122] canker-blossom – blossom eaten by a canker worm
[123] counterfeit – feigning, deceitful

HELENA
Good Hermia, do not be so bitter with me.
I evermore did love you, Hermia,
Did ever keep your counsels, never wrong'd you;
Save that, in love unto Demetrius,
I told him of your stealth unto this wood. 175
He follow'd you; for love I follow'd him;
And follow you no further. Let me go.

HERMIA
Why, get you gone: who is't that hinders you?

HELENA
A foolish heart, that I leave here behind.

HERMIA
What, with Lysander?

HELENA
                With Demetrius. 180

LYSANDER
Be not afraid; she shall not harm thee, Helena.

DEMETRIUS
No, sir, she shall not, though you take her part.

HELENA
O, when she's angry, she is keen and shrewd!
She was a vixen[124] when she went to school;
And though she be but little, she is fierce. 185

HERMIA
'Little' again! nothing but 'low' and 'little'!
Why will you suffer her to flout[125] me thus?
Let me come to her!

LYSANDER
                Get you gone, you dwarf;
You minimus,[126] of hindering knot-grass[127] made;
You bead, you acorn. 190

---

[124] vixen – quarrelsome girl
[125] flout – mock, make a fool of
[126] minimus – anything very small
[127] knot-grass – a British weed which is supposed to hinder growth

DEMETRIUS

Let her alone: speak not of Helena;
Take not her part; for, if thou dost intend
Never so little show of love to her,
Thou shalt aby[128] it.

LYSANDER
                    Now she holds me not;
Now follow, if thou darest, to try whose right,   195
Of thine or mine, is most in Helena.

DEMETRIUS
Follow? Nay, I'll go with thee, cheek by jowl.[129]

Exeunt LYSANDER and DEMETRIUS

HERMIA
You, mistress, all this coil is 'long[130] of you.
Nay, go not back.

HELENA
                I will not trust you, I,
Nor longer stay in your curst company.   200
Your hands than mine are quicker for a fray,[131]
My legs are longer though, to run away.

Exit HELENA

HERMIA
I am amazed, and know not what to say.

Exit HERMIA

OBERON
This is thy negligence.

---

[128] aby – pay, answer, atone
[129] cheek by jowl – close
[130] 'long – the fault of, owing to
[131] fray – fight

PUCK
Believe me, king of shadows, I mistook. 205
Did not you tell me I should know the man
By the Athenian garments he had on?

OBERON
Thou see'st these lovers seek a place to fight:
Hie therefore, Robin, overcast[132] the night;
And lead these testy rivals so astray 210
As one come not within another's way.
I'll to my queen and beg her Indian boy;
And then I will her charmed eye release
From monster's view, and all things shall be peace.

PUCK
My fairy lord, this must be done with haste, 215
For night's swift dragons[133] cut[134] the clouds full fast.

OBERON
Haste, make no delay;
We may effect this business yet ere day.

Exit

PUCK
Up and down, up and down,
I will lead them up and down: 220
Here comes one.

Re-enter LYSANDER

LYSANDER
Where art thou, proud Demetrius? Speak thou now.

PUCK
Here, villain, drawn and ready. Where art thou?

LYSANDER
I will be with thee straight.

---

[132] overcast – to darken over
[133] swift dragons – dragons drawing a chariot to bring forth the night
[134] cut – divide by passing through

PUCK
                              Follow me, then
To plainer ground.

Exit LYSANDER, as following the voice
Re-enter DEMETRIUS

DEMETRIUS
                    Lysander, speak again.   225
Thou runaway, thou coward, art thou fled?
Speak! In some bush? Where dost thou hide thy head?

PUCK
Thou coward, art thou bragging to the stars,
And wilt not come?

DEMETRIUS
                    Yea, art thou there?

PUCK
Follow my voice: we'll try no manhood here.   230

Exit DEMETRIUS
Re-enter LYSANDER

LYSANDER
When I come where he calls, then he is gone.
The villain is much lighter-heel'd than I:
I follow'd fast, but faster he did fly.

Lies down and sleeps
Re-enter PUCK and DEMETRIUS

PUCK
Ho, ho, ho! Coward, why comest thou not?

DEMETRIUS
Thou runn'st before me, shifting every place,   235
And darest not stand, nor look me in the face.
Where art thou now?

PUCK
                    Come hither; I am here.

DEMETRIUS
Nay, then, thou mock'st me. Thou shalt buy this dear
If ever I thy face by daylight see:
Now, go thy way. 240

Exhausted, lies down and sleeps
Re-enter HELENA

HELENA
O weary night, O long and tedious night,
Steal me[135] awhile from mine own company.

Lies down and sleeps

PUCK
Yet but three? Come one more;
Two of both kinds make up four.
Here she comes, curst and sad: 245
Cupid is a knavish lad,[136]
Thus to make poor females mad.

Re-enter HERMIA

HERMIA
Never so weary, never so in woe,
I can no further crawl, no further go;
Here will I rest me till the break of day. 250
Heavens shield Lysander, if they mean a fray!

Lies down and sleeps

PUCK
On the ground
Sleep sound:
I'll apply
To your eye, 255
Gentle lover, remedy.
(*Squeezing the juice on LYSANDER's eyes*)
When thou wakest,

[135] steal me – take secretly and without right
[136] knavish lad – villainous and wicked boy

Thou takest
True delight
In the sight   260
Of thy former lady's eye:
The man shall have his mare[137] again, and all shall be well.

Exit

ACT IV, SCENE I. The same.
LYSANDER, DEMETRIUS, HELENA, and HERMIA lying asleep. Enter TITANIA and BOTTOM; PEASEBLOSSOM, COBWEB, MOTH, MUSTARDSEED, and other Fairies; OBERON behind unseen

TITANIA
Come, sit thee down upon this flowery bed,
While I thy amiable cheeks do coy,[138]
And kiss thy fair large ears, my gentle joy.

BOTTOM
Where's Peaseblossom?

PEASEBLOSSOM
Ready.   5

BOTTOM
Scratch my head Peaseblossom. Where's Mounsieur Cobweb?

COBWEB
Ready.

BOTTOM
Mounsieur Cobweb, good mounsieur, get you your weapons
in your hand, and kill me a humble-bee; and, good mounsieur,
bring me the honey-bag; and, good mounsieur, have a care the   10
honey-bag break not. Where's Mounsieur Mustardseed?

MUSTARDSEED
What's your will?

BOTTOM
Nothing, good mounsieur, but to help Peaseblossom to scratch.

---

[137] mare – female horse – "all shall be right again"
[138] coy – stroke softly, caress

TITANIA
Oh say, sweet love, what thou desirest to eat.

BOTTOM
Truly, I could munch your good dry oats. Methinks I have a great desire to a bottle of hay. But, I pray you, let none of your people stir me: I have an exposition of sleep come upon me.

TITANIA
Sleep thou, and I will wind thee in my arms.
Fairies, begone, and be all ways away.[139]

Exeunt Fairies

O, how I love thee! How I dote on thee!

They sleep
Enter PUCK

OBERON
(*Advancing*)
Welcome, good Robin. See'st thou this sweet sight?
Her dotage[140] now I do begin to pity.
Gentle Puck, take this transformed scalp
From off the head of this Athenian swain;[141]
That he awaking when the other do
And think no more of this night's accidents
But as the fierce vexation[142] of a dream.
But first I will release the fairy queen.
(*Squeezing juice on her eyelids*)
Be as thou wast wont to be;
See as thou wast wont to see:
Now, my Titania; wake you, my sweet queen.

TITANIA
(*Waking*) My Oberon! what visions have I seen!
Methought I was enamour'd of an ass.

---

[139] be all ways away – be gone in every direction
[140] dotage – fondness
[141] swain – any person of low rank
[142] vexation – agitation, affliction in mind

OBERON
There lies your love.

TITANIA
How came these things to pass?
O, how mine eyes do loathe his visage[143] now! 35

OBERON
Silence awhile. Robin, take off this head.

PUCK removes the ass-head from BOTTOM

PUCK
Now, when thou wakest, with thine own fool's eyes peep.

OBERON
Come, my queen, take hands with me,
Now thou and I are new in amity,[144]
And will to-morrow midnight solemnly[145] 40
Dance in Duke Theseus' house triumphantly,
And bless it to all fair prosperity.

PUCK
Fairy king, attend, and mark:
I do hear the morning lark.

TITANIA
Come, my lord, and in our flight 45
Tell me how it came this night
That I sleeping here was found
With these mortals on the ground.

Exeunt
The four lovers and BOTTOM still lie asleep
Enter THESEUS, EGEUS, and train

THESEUS
But, soft, what nymphs are these?

EGEUS
My lord, this is my daughter here asleep; 50
And this, Lysander; this Demetrius is;

---

[143] visage – appearance, face, countenance
[144] amity – friendship, good understanding
[145] solemnly – formally, ceremoniously

This Helena.
I wonder of their being here together.

THESEUS
No doubt they rose up early to observe
The rite of May,[146] and hearing our intent,   55
Came here in grace[147] of our solemnity.
But speak, Egeus; is not this the day
That Hermia should give answer of her choice?

EGEUS
It is, my lord.

THESEUS
Good morrow, friends.   60

LYSANDER, DEMETRIUS, HELENA, and HERMIA wake

LYSANDER
Pardon, my lord.

THESEUS
                    I pray you all, stand up.
I know you two are rival enemies:
How comes this gentle concord[148] in the world?

LYSANDER
My lord, I shall reply amazedly,
I cannot truly say how I came here.   65
I came with Hermia hither; our intent
Was to be gone from Athens, where we might,
Without the peril of the Athenian law –

EGEUS
Enough, enough, my lord; you have enough:
I beg the law, the law, upon his head.   70
They would have stolen away; they would, Demetrius,
Thereby to have defeated you and me.

DEMETRIUS
My lord, fair Helen told me of their stealth,
Of this their purpose hither to this wood;

---

[146] rite of May – festivities celebrating May Day
[147] grace – in honor
[148] concord – agreement of minds

And I in fury hither follow'd them, 75
Fair Helena in fancy following me.
But, by some power it is, my love to Hermia,
Melted as the snow; and all the faith,
The object and the pleasure of mine eye,
Is only Helena. To her, my lord, 80
Was I betroth'd ere I saw Hermia.

THESEUS
Fair lovers, you are fortunately met:
Egeus, I will overbear your will;
For in the temple by and by with us
These couples shall eternally be knit. 85

Exeunt THESEUS, EGEUS, and train

HELENA
Methinks I have found Demetrius like a jewel,
Mine own, and not mine own.

DEMETRIUS
                        Are you sure
That we are awake? It seems to me
That yet we sleep, we dream. Do not you think
The Duke was here, and bid us follow him? 90

HERMIA
Yea; and my father.

LYSANDER
And he did bid us follow to the temple.

DEMETRIUS
Why, then, we are awake: let's follow him
And by the way let us recount our dreams.

Exeunt

BOTTOM
(*Awaking*) When my cue comes, call me, and I will answer: 95
my next is, 'Most fair Pyramus'. Heigh-ho! Peter Quince!
Flute, the bellows-mender! Snout, the tinker! Starveling! God's
my life, stolen hence, and left me asleep! I have had a most rare

vision. I have had a dream, past the wit of man to say what dream
it was: man is but an ass, if he go about to expound this dream. 100
Methought I was, there is no man can tell what. Methought I
was, – and methought I had, – but man is but a patched[149] fool, if
he will offer to say what methought I had. The eye of man hath not
heard, the ear of man hath not seen, man's hand is not able to taste,
his tongue to conceive, nor his heart to report, what my dream 105
was. I will get Peter Quince to write a ballad of this dream: it shall
be called Bottom's Dream, because it hath no bottom; and I will
sing it in the latter end of a play, before the duke: peradventure,[150]
to make it the more gracious, I shall sing it at her death.

Exit

ACT IV, SCENE II. Athens. QUINCE's house.
Enter QUINCE, FLUTE, SNOUT, and STARVELING

QUINCE
Have you sent to Bottom's house? Is he come home yet?

STARVELING
He cannot be heard of. Out of doubt he is transported.

FLUTE
If he come not, then the play is marred: it goes not forward, doth it?

QUINCE
It is not possible: you have not a man in all Athens able to
discharge Pyramus but he. 5

FLUTE
No, he hath simply the best wit of any handicraft man in Athens.

Enter SNUG

SNUG
Masters, the Duke is coming from the temple, and there is two
or three lords and ladies more married: if our sport had gone
forward, we had all been made men.[151]

---
[149] patched – small, paltry
[150] peradventure – perhaps
[151] made men – having one's fortune made, fortunate

Enter BOTTOM

BOTTOM
Where are these lads? Where are these hearts? 10

QUINCE
Bottom! O most courageous day! O most happy hour!

BOTTOM
Masters, I am to discourse wonders: but ask me not what; for if I tell you, I am no true Athenian. I will tell you every thing, right as it fell out.

QUINCE
Let us hear, sweet Bottom.

BOTTOM
Not a word of me. All that I will tell you is, that the Duke hath 15
dined. Get your apparel together; meet presently at the palace; every man look o'er his part; for the short and the long is, our play is preferred. No more words: away! go, away!

Exeunt

ACT V, SCENE I. Athens. The palace of THESEUS.
Enter THESEUS, PHILOSTRATE, Lords and Attendants

THESEUS
Here come the lovers, full of joy and mirth.

Enter LYSANDER, DEMETRIUS, HERMIA, and HELENA

Joy, gentle friends, joy and fresh days of love
Accompany your hearts!

LYSANDER
     More than to us
Wait in your royal walks, your board,[152] your bed!

---

[152] board – table

THESEUS
Come now; what masques, what dances shall we have?　　5
Where is our usual manager of mirth?
What revels are in hand? Is there no play?
Call Philostrate.

PHILOSTRATE
　　　　Here, mighty Theseus.

THESEUS
Say, what abridgement[153] have you for this evening?

PHILOSTRATE
There is a brief[154] how many sports are ripe:[155]　　10
Make choice of which your highness will see first.

Giving a paper

THESEUS
(*Reads*) 'A tedious brief scene of young Pyramus
And his love Thisbe; very tragical mirth'.
Merry and tragical? Tedious and brief?

PHILOSTRATE
A play there is, my lord, some ten words long,　　15
Which is as brief as I have known a play;
But by ten words, my lord, it is too long,
Which makes it tedious.

THESEUS
What are they that do play it?

PHILOSTRATE
Hard-handed men that work in Athens here,　　20
Which never labour'd in their minds till now,
And now have toil'd their unbreathed memories
With this same play, against your nuptial
To do you service.

[153] abridgement – pastime
[154] brief – summary
[155] ripe – prepared

THESEUS
                And we will hear it.
Go, bring them in: and take your places.   25

PHILOSTRATE
So please your Grace, the Prologue is address'd.

THESEUS
Let him approach.

Flourish of trumpets – Enter QUINCE for the Prologue

Prologue
If we offend, it is with our good will.
That you should think, we come not to offend,
But with good will. To show our simple skill,   30
That is the true beginning of our end.
The actors are at hand; and by their show
You shall know all that you are like to know.

Enter PYRAMUS and THISBE, WALL, MOONSHINE, and LION

Gentles, perchance you wonder at this show;
But wonder on, till truth make all things plain.   35
This man is Pyramus, if you would know;
This beauteous lady Thisbe is certain.
This man, with lime and rough-cast,[156] *doth present*
Wall, and through Wall's chink they are content
To whisper. At the which let no man wonder.   40
This man, with lanthorn, dog, and bush of thorn,
Presenteth Moonshine. This grisly beast is Lion.

Exeunt PROLOGUE, PYRAMUS, THISBE, LION, and MOONSHINE

Wall
In this same interlude it doth befall
That I, one Snout by name, present a wall;
Through which the lovers, Pyramus and Thisbe,   45
Did whisper often very secretly.

---

[156] rough-cast – plaster mixed with pebbles

Enter PYRAMUS

Pyramus
O grim-look'd night! O night with hue so black!
O night, which ever art when day is not!
O night, O night! alack, alack, alack,
I fear my Thisbe's promise is forgot! 50
And thou, O wall, O sweet, O lovely wall,
Show me thy chink,[157] *to blink*[158] *through with mine eyne!*

(WALL holds up his fingers)

Thanks, courteous wall: Jove shield thee well for this!
But what see I? No Thisbe do I see.
O wicked wall, through whom I see no bliss! 55
Cursed be thy stones for thus deceiving me!

Enter THISBE

Thisbe
O wall, full often hast thou heard my moans,
For parting my fair Pyramus and me!
My cherry lips have often kiss'd thy stones,
Thy stones with lime and hair knit up in thee. 60

Pyramus
I see a voice: now will I to the chink,
To spy an I can hear my Thisbe's face.
Thisbe!

Thisbe
    My love thou art, my love I think!

Pyramus
Think what thou wilt, I am thy lover's grace;
O kiss me through the hole of this vile wall! 65

Thisbe
I kiss the wall's hole, not your lips at all.

---

[157] chink – fissure, crack
[158] blink – flicker, twinkle with the eye

Pyramus
Wilt thou at Ninny's tomb meet me straightway?

Thisbe
'Tide[159] *life, 'tide death, I come without delay.*

Exeunt PYRAMUS and THISBE

Wall
Thus have I, Wall, my part discharged so;
And, being done, thus Wall away doth go. 70

Exit WALL
Enter LION and MOONSHINE

Lion
You, ladies, you, whose gentle hearts do fear
May now perchance both quake and tremble here,
When lion rough in wildest rage doth roar.
Then know that I, one Snug the joiner, am
A lion fell,[160] *nor else no lion's dam.*[161] 75

Moonshine
This lanthorn doth the horned moon present; –
This lanthorn doth the horned moon present;
Myself the man i' the moon do seem to be.

ALL
I am aweary of this moon: would he would change!

Moonshine
All that I have to say is, to tell you that the lanthorn is the moon; 80
I the Man in the Moon; this thorn-bush, my thorn-bush;
and this dog, my dog.

Enter THISBE

Thisbe
This is old Ninny's tomb. Where is my love?

---

[159] 'tide – betide, to happen, to befall
[160] fell – fierce, savage
[161] dam – female parent

Lion
(*Roaring*) O – !

THISBE runs off
The LION shakes Thisbe's mantle, and exits
Enter PYRAMUS

Pyramus
Sweet Moon, I thank thee for thy sunny beams; 85
I thank thee, Moon, for shining now so bright;
For, by thy gracious, golden, glittering gleams,
I trust to take of truest Thisbe sight.
But stay! O spite!
But mark, poor knight, 90
What dreadful dole is here!
Eyes, do you see?
How can it be?
O dainty duck! O dear!
Thy mantle[162] *good,* 95
What! Stain'd with blood!
Come, tears, confound!
Out, sword, and wound
The pap of Pyramus;
Ay, that left pap,[163] 100
Where heart doth hop:

(*Stabs himself*)

Thus die I, thus, thus, thus!
Now am I dead,
Now am I fled;
Moon take thy flight! 105

Exit MOONSHINE

Now die, die, die, die, die.

(*Dies*)
Re-enter THISBE

---
[162] mantle – cloak
[163] pap – the nipple of males

Thisbe
Asleep, my love?
What, dead, my dove?
O Pyramus, arise!
Speak, speak. Quite dumb? 110
Dead, dead? A tomb
Must cover thy sweet eyes.
These lily lips,
This cherry nose,
These yellow cowslip[164] *cheeks,* 115
Are gone, are gone:
Lovers, make moan:
Tongue, not a word:
Come, trusty sword;
Come, blade, my breast imbrue:[165] 120

(*Stabs herself*)

And, farewell, friends;
Thus Thisbe ends:
Adieu, adieu, adieu.

(*Dies*)

BOTTOM
(*Starting up*) Will it please you to see the epilogue?

PETER QUINCE (THESEUS)
No epilogue, I pray you; for your play needs no excuse. Never 125
excuse; for when the players are all dead, there needs none
to be blamed. Let your epilogue alone.

A dance

The iron tongue[166] of midnight hath told twelve.
Lovers, to bed; 'tis almost fairy time.

---

[164] cowslip – a type of primrose
[165] imbrue – to shed blood
[166] iron tongue – the clapper of a bell

I fear we shall out-sleep the coming morn 130
As much as we this night have overwatch'd.
Sweet friends, to bed.

Exeunt all
Enter PUCK

PUCK
Now the hungry lion roars,
And the wolf behowls[167] the moon;
Now it is the time of night 135
That the graves all gaping wide,
Every one lets forth his sprite
In the church-way paths to glide.
And we fairies, that do run
By the triple Hecate's team,[168] 140
From the presence of the sun,
Following darkness like a dream,
Now are frolic;[169] not a mouse
Shall disturb this hallow'd[170] house.
I am sent with broom before, 145
To sweep the dust behind the door.

Enter OBERON and TITANIA with their train

OBERON
Through the house give glimmering light,
By the dead and drowsy fire;
Every elf and fairy sprite
Hop as light as bird from brier. 150

TITANIA
Hand in hand, with fairy grace,
Will we sing, and bless this place.

Song and dance

---

[167] behowls – to howl at
[168] triple Hecate's team – alluding to her threefold character; in heaven, earth and below
[169] frolic – gay, merry
[170] hallow'd – made holy

OBERON
Now, until the break of day,
Through this house each fairy stray.
To the best bride-bed will we, 155
Which by us shall blessed be;
So shall all the couples three
Ever true in loving be;
With this field-dew consecrate,[171]
Every fairy take his gait;[172] 160
Trip away; make no stay;
Meet me all by break of day.

Exeunt OBERON, TITANIA, and train

PUCK
If we shadows have offended,
Think but this, and all is mended,
That you have but slumber'd here 165
While these visions did appear.
And this weak and idle theme,
No more yielding but a dream.
Gentles, do not reprehend:[173]
If you pardon, we will mend. 170
And, as I am an honest Puck,
If we have unearned luck
Now to 'scape[174] the serpent's tongue,[175]
We will make amends ere long;
Give me your hands, if we be friends, 175
And Robin shall restore amends.

Exit

---

[171] field-dew consecrate – to make sacred with dew taken from the field
[172] gait – marching
[173] reprehend – blame
[174] 'scape – escape, to avoid
[175] serpent's tongue – not to be hissed at

6
A MIDSUMMER NIGHT'S DREAM
Suggested cast list and character assignments for a small cast

<u>6 actors, gender flexible. Cast can also be as large as 23 actors.</u>

Actor 1 – Bottom, Theseus, Fairy (2.1, 2.2)
Actor 2 – Puck, Egeus, Peter Quince, Peaseblossom
Actor 3 – Hermia, Titania, Snout
Actor 4 – Lysander, Oberon, Starveling, Moth
Actor 5 – Demetrius, Flute, Cowbweb, Fairy (2.1, 2.2)
Actor 6 – Hippolyta, Helena, Snug, Mustardseed, Philostrate

7
TWO GENTLEMEN OF VERONA

William Shakespeare

Originally written – 1589–1593
First Published – 1623
First recorded performance – 1594–1595

*Edited and Abridged by Julie Fain Lawrence-Edsell
(adapted from http://shakespeare.mit.edu)*

Dramatis Personae

DUKE OF MILAN, father to Sylvia
VALENTINE, a young gentleman of Verona
PROTEUS, another gentleman of Verona
ANTONIO, father to Proteus
THURIO, suitor to Sylvia and rival to Valentine
EGLAMOUR, agent to Sylvia in her escape
SPEED, servant to Valentine
LAUNCE, servant to Proteus
CRAB, dog to Launce
~~**PANTHINO**, servant to Antonio~~…lines given to LAUNCE
~~**HOST**, where Julia lodges~~

JULIA, beloved of Proteus
SYLVIA, beautiful young woman of Milan
LUCETTA, waiting woman to Julia

Outlaws, servants, musicians

ACT I, SCENE I. Verona. An open place.
Enter VALENTINE and PROTEUS

VALENTINE
Cease to persuade, my loving Proteus:
Were't not affection chains[1] thy tender days
To the sweet glances of thy honour'd love,
I rather would entreat thy company
To see the wonders of the world abroad. 5
But since thou lovest, love still and thrive therein,
Even as I would when I to love begin.

PROTEUS
Wilt thou be gone? Sweet Valentine, adieu!
Think on thy Proteus, when thou haply seest
Some rare note-worthy object in thy travel. 10
If ever danger do environ[2] thee,
Commend thy grievance to my holy prayers,
For I will be thy beadsman,[3] Valentine.

VALENTINE
And on a love-book pray for my success?

PROTEUS
Upon some book I love I'll pray for thee. 15

VALENTINE
That's on some shallow story of deep love.

PROTEUS
'Tis love you cavil[4] at: I am not Love.[5]

VALENTINE
Love is your master, for he masters you:
And he that is so yoked[6] by a fool,
Methinks, should not be chronicled for wise. 20

---
[1] chains – binds
[2] environ – to surround
[3] beadsman – a man hired by another to pray for him
[4] cavil – to quarrel, to find fault
[5] Love – Cupid, the god of love
[6] yoked – subdued, brought into bondage

PROTEUS
Yet writers say, as in the sweetest bud
The eating canker[7] dwells, so eating love
Inhabits in the finest wits of all.

VALENTINE
But wherefore waste I time to counsel thee,
That art a votary[8] to fond desire! 25
Once more adieu! My father at the road
Expects my coming, there to see me shipp'd.

PROTEUS
And thither will I bring thee, Valentine.

VALENTINE
Sweet Proteus, no; now let us take our leave.
To Milan let me hear from thee by letters 30
Of thy success in love – and what news else,
And likewise will visit thee with mine.

PROTEUS
All happiness bechance[9] to thee in Milan!

VALENTINE
As much to you at home! and so, farewell.

Exit

PROTEUS
He after honour hunts, I after love: 35
I leave myself, my friends and all, for love.
Thou, Julia, thou hast metamorphosed[10] me,
Made me neglect my studies, lose my time,
War with good counsel, set the world at nought;[11]
Made wit with musing[12] weak, heart sick with thought. 40

---

[7] canker – a worm that preys upon blossoms
[8] votary – one who has taken a vow
[9] bechance – to befall, to happen to
[10] metamorphosed – changed into a different form
[11] at nought – to despise, to slight
[12] musing – deep thinking on things of a painful nature

Enter SPEED

SPEED
Sir Proteus, save you! Saw you my master?

PROTEUS
But now he parted hence, to embark for Milan.

SPEED
Twenty to one then he is shipp'd already,
And I have play'd the sheep in losing him.

PROTEUS
True; and thy master a shepherd. 45

SPEED
The shepherd seeks the sheep, and not the sheep the shepherd;
but I seek my master, and my master seeks not me: therefore I
am no sheep.

PROTEUS
The sheep for fodder[13] follow the shepherd; the shepherd for
food follows not the sheep: thou for wages followest thy master; 50
thy master for wages follows not thee: therefore thou art a sheep.

SPEED
Such another proof will make me cry 'baa'.

PROTEUS
But, dost thou hear? gavest thou my letter to Julia?

SPEED
Ay sir: I, a lost mutton,[14] gave your letter to her, a laced mutton,[15]
and she, a laced mutton, gave me, a lost mutton, nothing for 55
my labour.

PROTEUS
Beshrew me, but you have a quick wit.

SPEED
And yet it cannot overtake your slow purse.[16]

---

[13] fodder – food for sheep
[14] mutton – sheep
[15] laced mutton – prostitute, female flesh
[16] slow purse – money bag not opened quick enough for payment

PROTEUS
Come come, open the matter in brief: what said she?

SPEED
Open your purse, that the money and the matter may be both at once delivered.

PROTEUS
Well, sir, here is for your pains. What said she?

SPEED
Truly, sir, I think you'll hardly win her.

PROTEUS
Why, couldst thou perceive so much from her?

SPEED
Sir, I could perceive nothing at all from her; no, not so much as a ducat[17] for delivering your letter: and being so hard[18] to me that brought your mind, I fear she'll prove as hard to you in telling your mind.

PROTEUS
What said she? nothing?

SPEED
No, not so much as 'Take this for thy pains'; in requital[19] whereof, carry your letters yourself: and so, sir, I'll commend you to my master.

PROTEUS
Go, go, be gone, to save your ship from wreck.

Exit SPEED

I must go send some better messenger:
I fear my Julia would not deign[20] my lines,
Receiving them from such a worthless post.[21]

Exit

---

[17] ducat – gold coin
[18] hard – unfeeling, cruel
[19] requital – reward
[20] deign – to condescend to take, not to distain
[21] post – messenger

ACT I, SCENE II. The same. Garden of JULIA's house.
Enter JULIA and LUCETTA

JULIA
But say, Lucetta, now we are alone,
Wouldst thou then counsel me to fall in love?

LUCETTA
Ay, madam, so you stumble not unheedfully.[22]

JULIA
Of all the fair resort[23] of gentlemen
In thy opinion which is worthiest love?   5

LUCETTA
Please you repeat their names, I'll show my mind
According to my shallow simple skill.

JULIA
What think'st thou of the fair Sir Eglamour?

LUCETTA
As of a knight well-spoken, neat and fine;
But, were I you, he never should be mine.   10

JULIA
What think'st thou of the rich Mercatio?

LUCETTA
Well of his wealth; but of himself, so so.

JULIA
What think'st thou of the gentle Proteus?

LUCETTA
Lord, Lord! to see what folly[24] reigns in us!

---

[22] unheedfully – inconsiderately
[23] resort – visits made to talk
[24] folly – absurd act

JULIA
How now! what means this passion at his name? 15

LUCETTA
Pardon, dear madam: 'tis a passing shame
That I, unworthy body as I am,
Should censure[25] thus on lovely gentlemen.

JULIA
Why not on Proteus, as of all the rest?

LUCETTA
Then thus; of many good I think him best. 20

JULIA
And wouldst thou have me cast my love on him?

LUCETTA
Ay, if you thought your love not cast away.

JULIA
Why he, of all the rest, hath never moved me.

LUCETTA
Yet he, of all the rest, I think, best loves ye.

JULIA
His little speaking shows his love but small. 25

LUCETTA
Fire that's closest kept burns most of all.

JULIA
I would I knew his mind.

LUCETTA
Peruse this paper, madam.

JULIA
'To Julia'. Say, from whom?

LUCETTA
That the contents will show. 30

JULIA
Say, say, who gave it thee?

---
[25] censure – to judge

LUCETTA
Sir Valentine's page; and sent, I think, from Proteus.
He would have given it you; but I, being in the way,
Did in your name receive it: pardon the fault I pray.

JULIA
Now, by my modesty, a goodly broker![26]   35
Dare you presume to harbour wanton lines?[27]
To whisper and conspire against my youth?
There. Take the paper.

She gives the letter to Lucetta

              See it be returned.
Will ye be gone?

LUCETTA
           That you may ruminate.[28]

Exit

JULIA
And yet I would I had o'erlooked the letter: 40
It were a shame to call her back again
And pray her[29] to a fault for which I chid[30] her.
What a fool is she, that knows I am a maid,
And would not force the letter to my view!
What ho! Lucetta!

Re-enter LUCETTA

LUCETTA
         What would your ladyship?   45

LUCETTA drops and picks up the letter

JULIA
What is't that you took up so gingerly?

---
[26] broker – agent, negotiator
[27] wanton lines – frivolous and insignificant words
[28] ruminate – ponder
[29] pray her – ask earnestly, entreat her
[30] chid – scolded

LUCETTA
Nothing.

JULIA
Why didst thou stoop, then?

LUCETTA
To take a paper up that I let fall.

JULIA
And is that paper nothing? 50

LUCETTA
Nothing concerning me.

JULIA
Then let it lie for those that it concerns.

LUCETTA
Madam, it will not lie where it concerns
Unless it have a false interpreter.

JULIA
This babble[31] shall not henceforth trouble me. 55
Here is a coil[32] with protestation!

Tears the letter

Go get you gone, and let the papers lie:
You would be fingering them, to anger me.

LUCETTA
(*Aside*) She makes it strange; but she would be best pleased
To be so anger'd with another letter. 60

Exit LUCETTA

JULIA
O hateful hands, to tear such loving words!
Injurious wasps, to feed on such sweet honey
And kill the bees that yield it with your stings!
I'll kiss each several paper for amends.

---

[31] babble – foolish talk
[32] coil – turmoil, confusion

Look, here is writ 'kind Julia'. Unkind Julia! 65
And here is writ 'love-wounded Proteus'.
Poor wounded name, my bosom as a bed
Shall lodge thee till thy wound be thoroughly heal'd;
Be calm, good wind, blow not a word away
Till I have found each letter in the letter, 70
Except mine own name: that some whirlwind bear
Unto a ragged fearful-hanging rock
And throw it thence into the raging sea!
Lo, here in one line is his name twice writ,
'Poor forlorn Proteus, passionate Proteus, 75
To the sweet Julia': that I'll tear away.
And yet I will not, sith so prettily
He couples it to his complaining names.
Thus will I fold them one on another:
Now kiss, embrace, contend,[33] do what you will. 80

Re-enter LUCETTA

LUCETTA
Madam, dinner is ready, and your father stays.

JULIA
Well, let us go.

LUCETTA
What, shall these papers lie like tell-tales[34] here?

JULIA
If you respect them, best to take them up.

LUCETTA
Nay, I was taken up[35] for laying them down: 85
Yet here they shall not lie, for catching cold.

JULIA
Come, come; will't please you go?

Exeunt

---

[33] contend – quarrel, fight
[34] tell-tales – a person or thing that gives troublesome information about others
[35] taken up – scolded

ACT I, SCENE III. The same. ANTONIO's house.
Enter ANTONIO and PROTEUS

PROTEUS
Sweet love! sweet lines! sweet life!
Here is her hand, the agent of her heart;
Here is her oath for love, her honour's pawn.[36]
O, that our fathers would applaud our loves,
To seal our happiness with their consents!   5
O heavenly Julia!

ANTONIO
How now! what letter are you reading there?

PROTEUS
May't please your lordship, 'tis a word or two
Of commendations[37] sent from Valentine,
Deliver'd by a friend that came from him.   10

ANTONIO
Lend me the letter; let me see what news.

PROTEUS
There is no news, my lord, but that he writes
How happily he lives, how well beloved;
Wishing me with him, partner of his fortune.

ANTONIO
And how stand you affected to his wish?   15

PROTEUS
As one relying on your lordship's will.

ANTONIO
My will is something sorted[38] with his wish.
I am resolved that thou shalt spend some time
With Valentinus in the emperor's court:
Tomorrow be in readiness to go.   20

---

[36] pawn — something given as a pledge
[37] commendations — greetings
[38] something sorted — adapted to

PROTEUS
My lord, I cannot be so soon provided:
Please you, deliberate a day or two.

ANTONIO
Look, what thou want'st shall be sent after thee:
No more of stay. Tomorrow thou must go.

Exit ANTONIO

PROTEUS
Thus have I shunn'd the fire for fear of burning,   25
And drench'd me in the sea, where I am drown'd.
I fear'd to show my father Julia's letter,
Lest he should take exceptions to my love;
And with the vantage of mine own excuse
Hath he excepted most against my love.   30

Exit

ACT II, SCENE I. Milan. The DUKE's palace.
Enter VALENTINE and SPEED

VALENTINE
Ah, Silvia, Silvia!

SPEED
Madam Silvia! Madam Silvia!

VALENTINE
Why, sir, who bade you call her?

SPEED
Your worship, sir, or else I mistook.

VALENTINE
Go to, sir. Tell me, do you know Madam Silvia?   5

SPEED
She that your worship loves?

VALENTINE
Why, how know you that I am in love?

SPEED
Marry, by these special marks: to relish[39] a love-song; to walk
alone; to sigh; to weep; to fast; to watch like one that fears robbing;
– now you are metamorphosed with a mistress, that, when I look   10
on you, I can hardly think you my master.

VALENTINE
But tell me, dost thou know my lady Silvia?

SPEED
She that you gaze on so as she sits at supper? Why, sir, I know her not.

VALENTINE
Dost thou know her by my gazing on her, and yet knowest her not?

SPEED
Is she not hard-favoured,[40] sir?   15

VALENTINE
Not so fair, boy, as well favoured.

SPEED
You never saw her since she was deformed.

VALENTINE
How long hath she been deformed?

SPEED
Ever since you loved her.

VALENTINE
I have loved her ever since I saw her; and still I see her beautiful.   20

SPEED
If you love her, you cannot see her.

VALENTINE
Why?

SPEED
Because Love is blind. O, that you had mine eyes – you, being
in love, cannot see to put on your hose.

---

[39] relish – to like or be pleased with, to serve up as something pleasing
[40] hard-favoured – ill looking, ugly

VALENTINE
Belike, boy, then, you are in love; for last morning you could   25
not see to wipe my shoes.

SPEED
True, sir; I was in love with my bed

VALENTINE
Last night she enjoined[41] me to write some lines to one she loves.

SPEED
And have you?

VALENTINE
I have.   30

SPEED
Are they not lamely writ?

VALENTINE
No, boy, but as well as I can do them. Peace! here she comes.

SPEED
(*Aside*) O excellent motion! O exceeding puppet![42] Now will he interpret to[43] her.

Enter SILVIA

VALENTINE
Madam and mistress, a thousand good-morrows.   35

SILVIA
Sir Valentine and servant, to you two thousand.

VALENTINE
As you enjoin'd me, I have writ your letter
Unto the secret nameless friend of yours.

SILVIA
I thank you gentle servant: 'tis very clerkly[44] done.

---

[41] enjoined – ordered, charged
[42] puppet – doll, small figure made to play with
[43] interpret to – to play the interpreter, decipherer, explainer
[44] clerkly – with great penmanship

VALENTINE
Now trust me, madam, it came hardly[45] off; 40
For being ignorant to whom it goes
I writ at random, very doubtfully.

SILVIA
A pretty period! Well, I guess the sequel;
And yet I will not name it; and yet I care not;
And yet take this again; and yet I thank you, 45
Meaning henceforth to trouble you no more.

VALENTINE
What means your ladyship? Do you not like it?

SILVIA
Yes, yes; the lines are very quaintly writ;
But since unwillingly, take them again.
Nay, take them.

VALENTINE
    Madam, they are for you. 50

SILVIA
Ay, ay; you writ them, sir, at my request;
But I will none of them; they are for you;
I would have had them writ more movingly.

VALENTINE
Please you, I'll write your ladyship another.

SILVIA
And when it's writ, for my sake read it over, 55
And if it please you, so. If not, why, so.

VALENTINE
If it please me, madam, what then?

SILVIA
Why, if it please you, take it for your labour:
And so, good morrow, servant.

Exit

---

[45] hardly – with difficulty

SPEED
O jest[46] unseen, inscrutable,[47] invisible, 60
My master sues[48] to her, and she hath taught her suitor,
He being her pupil, to become her tutor.
O excellent device![49] Was there ever heard a better,
That my master, being scribe,[50] to himself should write the letter?

VALENTINE
How now, sir, what are you reasoning with yourself? 65

SPEED
'Tis you that have the reason. Why, she woos[51] you by a figure.

VALENTINE
What figure?

SPEED
By a letter, I should say.

VALENTINE
Why, she hath not writ to me?

SPEED
What need she, when she hath made you write to yourself? 70
Why, do you not perceive the jest?

VALENTINE
No, believe me.

SPEED
Why, she hath given you a letter.

VALENTINE
That's the letter I writ to her friend.

SPEED
And that letter hath she delivered, and there an end. Why muse[52] 75
you, sir? 'Tis dinner-time.

---

[46] jest – ridiculous and amusing act
[47] inscrutable – impenetrable, not to be understood
[48] sues – petitions, begs
[49] device – strategy, contrivance
[50] scribe – one who writes down something
[51] woos – solicit in love
[52] muse – give one's self up to thought of a painful nature

VALENTINE
I have dined.

SPEED
Sir, though the chameleon Love can feed on the air, I am one that am nourished by my victuals,[53] and would fain[54] have meat.

Exeunt

ACT II, SCENE II. Verona. JULIA's house.
Enter PROTEUS and JULIA

PROTEUS
Have patience, gentle Julia.

JULIA
I must, where is no remedy.

PROTEUS
When possibly I can, I will return.

JULIA
If you turn not, you will return the sooner.
Keep this remembrance for thy Julia's sake. 5

Giving a ring

PROTEUS
Why then, we'll make exchange; here, take you this.

JULIA
And seal the bargain with a holy kiss.

PROTEUS
Here is my hand for my true constancy;
And when that hour o'erslips me in the day
Wherein I sigh not, Julia, for thy sake, 10
The next ensuing hour some foul mischance
Torment me for my love's forgetfulness!
Julia, farewell!

Exit JULIA

---

[53] victuals – food, provisions
[54] fain – gladly, willingly

What, gone without a word?
Ay, so true love should do: it cannot speak.

Enter LAUNCE

LAUNCE
Sir Proteus, you are stay'd for.[55] 15

PROTEUS
Go; I come, I come.
Alas! this parting strikes poor lovers dumb.[56]

Exeunt

ACT II, SCENE III. The same. A street.
Enter LAUNCE, leading a dog

LAUNCE
Nay, 'twill be this hour ere I have done weeping; I have received my proportion[57] and am going with Sir Proteus to the Imperial's court. I think Crab, my dog, be the sourest-natured dog that lives: my mother weeping, my father wailing, my sister crying, our maid howling, our cat wringing her hands, and all our house in a great 5
perplexity,[58] yet did not this cruel-hearted cur[59] shed one tear: he is a stone, a very pebble stone, and has no more pity in him than a dog. Nay, I'll show you the manner of it. This shoe is my father: no, this left shoe is my father: no, no, this left shoe is my mother, yes, it is so, it is so, it hath the worser sole and this my father: now, 10
this staff is my sister and I am the dog: no, the dog is himself, and I am the dog, Oh! the dog is me, and I am myself; ay, so, so. Now come I to my father; Father, your blessing: now should I kiss my father; well, he weeps on. Now come I to my mother: well, I kiss her; why, there 'tis; here's my mother's breath up and down. 15
Now come I to my sister; mark the moan she makes. Now the dog all this while sheds not a tear nor speaks a word; but see how I lay the dust with my tears…My master is shipped. Well, I will go.

Exeunt

---

[55] stay'd for – waited for
[56] dumb – at a loss for words
[57] proportion – allotment, fortune
[58] perplexity – bewilderment
[59] cur – term of contempt for a dog

ACT II, SCENE IV. Milan. The DUKE's palace.
Enter SILVIA, VALENTINE

SILVIA
Servant!

VALENTINE
Mistress?

SILVIA
Servant, you are sad.

VALENTINE
Indeed, madam, I seem so. Haply I do.

SILVIA
No more, gentleman, no more. Here comes my father. 5

Enter DUKE

DUKE
Now, daughter Silvia, you are hard beset.
Sir Valentine, your father's in good health:
What say you to a letter from your friends
Of much good news?

VALENTINE
　　　　　　　My lord, I will be thankful.
To any happy messenger from thence. 10

DUKE
Know ye Don Antonio, your countryman?

VALENTINE
Ay, my good lord, I know the gentleman.

DUKE
Hath he not a son?

VALENTINE
Ay, my good lord; a son that well deserves
The honour and regard of such a father. 15

DUKE
You know him well?

VALENTINE
I know him as myself, for from our infancy
We have conversed and spent our hours together:
Yet hath Sir Proteus, for that's his name,
Made use and fair advantage of his days; 20
His years but young, but his experience old.

DUKE
Well, sir, this gentleman is come to me,
And here he means to spend his time awhile:
I think 'tis no unwelcome news to you.

VALENTINE
Should I have wish'd a thing, it had been he. 25

DUKE
Welcome him then according to his worth.
I will send him hither to you presently.

Exit

VALENTINE
This is the gentleman I told your ladyship
Had come along with me, but that his mistress
Did hold his eyes lock'd in her crystal[60] looks. 30

SILVIA
Belike that now she hath enfranchised[61] them
Upon some other pawn for fealty.[62]

VALENTINE
Nay, sure, I think she holds them prisoners still.

SILVIA
Nay, then he should be blind; and, being blind
How could he see his way to seek out you? 35

VALENTINE
Why, lady, Love hath twenty pair of eyes.

---

[60] crystal – bright eyes
[61] enfranchised – set at liberty, delivered
[62] pawn for fealty – pledge of loyalty

SILVIA
Have done, have done; here comes the gentleman.

Enter PROTEUS

VALENTINE
Welcome, dear Proteus! Mistress, I beseech you,
Confirm his welcome with some special favour.

SILVIA
His worth is warrant[63] for his welcome hither,
If this be he you oft have wish'd to hear from.

VALENTINE
Mistress, it is: sweet lady, entertain him
To be my fellow-servant to your ladyship.

SILVIA
Too low a mistress for so high a servant.

PROTEUS
Not so, sweet lady: but too mean[64] a servant
To have a look of such a worthy mistress.

VALENTINE
Sweet lady, entertain him for your servant.

PROTEUS
My duty will I boast of, nothing else.

SILVIA
Servant, you are welcome to a worthless mistress.

PROTEUS
I'll die on him that says so but yourself.

SILVIA
That you are welcome?

PROTEUS
              That you are worthless.

---

[63] warrant – surety, pledge
[64] mean – low, humble, poor

SILVIA
I'll leave you to confer⁶⁵ of home affairs.
When you have done, we look to hear from you.

PROTEUS
We'll both attend upon your ladyship.

Exeunt SILVIA

VALENTINE
Now, tell me, how do all from whence you came?   55

PROTEUS
Your friends are well and have them much commended.⁶⁶

VALENTINE
How does your lady, and how thrives your love?

PROTEUS
My tales of love were wont to weary you.
I know you joy not in a love discourse.

VALENTINE
Ay, Proteus, but that life is alter'd now.   60
O gentle Proteus, Love's a mighty lord,
And hath so humbled me as I confess,
There is no woe to his correction,
Nor to his service no such joy on earth.
Now, no discourse except it be of love.   65

PROTEUS
Enough; I read your fortune in your eye.
Was this the idol that you worship so?

VALENTINE
Even she; and is she not a heavenly saint?

PROTEUS
No, but she is an earthly paragon.⁶⁷

VALENTINE
Call her divine.

---

⁶⁵ confer – talk, discourse
⁶⁶ commended – recommend to remember
⁶⁷ paragon – something of supreme excellence

PROTEUS
                I will not flatter her.

VALENTINE
Then speak the truth by her; if not divine,
Yet let her be a principality,[68]
Sovereign to all the creatures on the earth.

PROTEUS
Except my mistress.

VALENTINE
                Sweet, except not any;
Except thou wilt except against my love.

PROTEUS
Have I not reason to prefer mine own?

VALENTINE
And I will help thee to prefer her too.
She shall be dignified with this high honour –
To bear my lady's train –
Pardon me, Proteus, all I can is nothing
To her whose worth makes other worthies nothing.
She is alone.

PROTEUS
         Then let her alone.

VALENTINE
Not for the world. Why, man, she is mine own,
And I as rich in having such a jewel.
My foolish rival, that her father likes
Only for his possessions are so huge,
Is gone with her along, and I must after,
For love, thou know'st, is full of jealousy.

PROTEUS
But she loves you?

VALENTINE
Ay, and we are betroth'd. Nay more, our marriage-hour,
With all the cunning manner of our flight,[69]

---

[68] principality – a person of the highest dignity, superior to other men
[69] flight – secret departure

Determined of; how I must climb her window,
The ladder made of cords, and all the means
Plotted and 'greed on for my happiness.
Good Proteus, go with me to my chamber, 95
In these affairs to aid me with thy counsel.

PROTEUS
I must unto the road, to disembark
Some necessaries that I needs must use,
And then I'll presently attend you.

VALENTINE
Will you make haste? 100

PROTEUS
I will.

Exit VALENTINE

Even as one heat another heat expels,
So the remembrance of my former love
Is by a newer object quite forgotten.
She is fair; and so is Julia that I love, 105
That I did love, for now my love is thaw'd;
Bears no impression of the thing it was.
Methinks my zeal[70] to Valentine is cold,
And that I love him not as I was wont.[71]
O, but I love his lady too too much, 110
And that's the reason I love him so little.
But when I look on her perfections,
There is no reason but I shall be blind.

(ACT II, V – cut and continue monologue in ACT II, VI)

To leave my Julia, shall I be forsworn;[72]
To love fair Silvia, shall I be forsworn; 115
To wrong my friend, I shall be much forsworn.
O sweet-suggesting Love, if thou hast sinned,

---
[70] zeal – intense and eager interest, strong enthusiasm in pursuit of a goal
[71] wont – accustomed
[72] forsworn – swear falsely, perjure one's self

Teach me, thy tempted subject, to excuse it!
At first I did adore a twinkling star,
But now I worship a celestial sun. 120
Julia I lose and Valentine I lose.
If I keep them, I needs must lose myself.
I will forget that Julia is alive,
Remembering that my love to her is dead;
And Valentine I'll hold an enemy, 125
Aiming at Silvia as a sweeter friend.
I cannot now prove constant to myself,
Without some treachery used to Valentine.
This night he meaneth with a corded ladder
To climb celestial Silvia's chamber-window, 130
Myself in counsel, his competitor.
Now presently I'll give her father notice
Who, all enraged, will banish Valentine;
For Thurio, he intends, shall wed his daughter.
But Valentine being gone, I'll quickly cross 135
By some sly trick blunt Thurio's dull proceeding.[73]
Love, lend me wings to make my purpose swift,
As thou hast lent me wit to plot this drift![74]

Exit

ACT II, SCENE VII. Verona. JULIA's house.
Enter JULIA and LUCETTA

JULIA
Counsel, Lucetta. Gentle girl, assist me.
How, with my honour, I may undertake
A journey to my loving Proteus.

LUCETTA
Alas, the way is wearisome and long!

JULIA
A true-devoted pilgrim[75] is not weary 5
To measure kingdoms with his feeble steps.
Much less shall she that hath Love's wings to fly,

---
[73] dull proceeding – awkward and stupid action
[74] drift – intention, aim, scheme
[75] pilgrim – one who travels to a holy place

And when the flight is made to one so dear,
Of such divine perfection, as Sir Proteus.

LUCETTA
Better forbear till Proteus make return. 10

JULIA
O, know'st thou not his looks are my soul's food?
Didst thou but know the inly touch of love,
Thou wouldst as soon go kindle fire with snow
As seek to quench the fire of love with words.

LUCETTA
I do not seek to quench your love's hot fire, 15
But qualify the fire's extreme rage.
But in what habit will you go along?

JULIA
Not like a woman; fit me with such weeds[76]
As may beseem some well-reputed page.[77]

LUCETTA
What fashion, madam shall I make your breeches?[78] 20

JULIA
Why even what fashion thou best likest, Lucetta.

LUCETTA
You must needs have them with a codpiece,[79] madam.

JULIA
Out, out, Lucetta! that would be ill-favour'd.
Lucetta, as thou lovest me, let me have
What thou thinkest meet[80] and is most mannerly. 25
But tell me, wench,[81] how will the world repute me
For undertaking so unstaid[82] a journey?
I fear me, it will make me scandalized.

---

[76] weeds – clothes
[77] page – a young boy attending on a person of distinction
[78] breeches – pants worn by males
[79] codpiece – conspicuous and decorative pouch covering male genitals, part of pants
[80] meet – proper, fit, answering the purpose
[81] wench – familiar term used for a woman, with tenderness or contempt
[82] unstaid – thoughtless, volatile

LUCETTA
If you think so, then stay at home and go not.

JULIA
Nay, that I will not. 30

LUCETTA
Then never dream on infamy,[83] but go.
If Proteus like your journey when you come,
I fear me, he will scarce be pleased withal.

JULIA
That is the least, Lucetta, of my fear.
A thousand oaths, an ocean of his tears 35
And instances of infinite of love
Warrant me welcome to my Proteus.

LUCETTA
Pray heaven he prove so, when you come to him!

JULIA
Now, as thou lovest me, do him not that wrong
To bear a hard opinion of his truth: 40
And presently go with me to my chamber,
To furnish[84] me upon my longing journey.
Come, answer not, but to it presently!
I am impatient of my tarriance.[85]

Exeunt

ACT III, SCENE I. Milan. The DUKE's palace.
Enter DUKE and PROTEUS

DUKE
Now, tell me, Proteus, what's your will with me?

PROTEUS
My gracious lord, that which I would discover[86]
The law of friendship bids me to conceal.
Know, worthy prince, Sir Valentine, my friend,

---
[83] infamy – disgrace
[84] furnish – supply with what is necessary
[85] tarriance – remaining in a place
[86] discover – reveal, betray

This night intends to steal away your daughter. 5
Myself am one made privy to the plot.
I know you have determined to bestow[87] her
On Thurio, whom your gentle daughter hates,
And should she thus be stol'n away from you,
It would be much vexation[88] to your age. 10
Thus, for my duty's sake, I rather chose
To cross[89] my friend in his intended drift
Than, by concealing it, heap on your head
A pack of sorrows which would press you down.

DUKE
Proteus, I thank thee for thine honest care. 15
This love of theirs myself have often seen,
Haply when they have judged me fast asleep,
And that thou mayst perceive my fear of this,
I nightly lodge her in an upper tower,
The key whereof myself have ever kept; 20
And thence she cannot be convey'd away.

PROTEUS
Know, noble lord, they have devised a mean
How he her chamber-window will ascend
And with a corded ladder fetch her down;
And this way comes he with it presently; 25
Where, if it please you, you may intercept him.
But, good my Lord, do it so cunningly
That my discovery be not aimed at.[90]

DUKE
Upon mine honour, he shall never know
That I had any light from thee of this. 30

PROTEUS
Adieu, my lord. Sir Valentine is coming.

Exit
Enter VALENTINE

---

[87] bestow – to grant, to give
[88] vexation – great uneasiness, grief
[89] cross – to hinder or thwart
[90] aimed at – suspected

DUKE
Sir Valentine, whither away so fast?

VALENTINE
Please it your grace, there is a messenger
That stays to bear my letters to my friends,
And I am going to deliver them. 35

DUKE
Be they of much import?

VALENTINE
The tenor[91] of them doth but signify
My health and happy being at your court.

DUKE
Nay then, no matter. Stay with me awhile;
I am to break[92] with thee of some affairs. 40
There is a lady in Verona here
Whom I affect, but she is nice and coy;
How and which way may I bestow myself
To be regarded in her sun-bright eye?

VALENTINE
Win her with gifts, if she respect not words. 45

DUKE
But she did scorn a present that I sent her.

VALENTINE
A woman sometimes scorns what best contents her.

DUKE
But she I mean is promised by her friends
Unto a youthful gentleman of worth,
And kept severely[93] from resort[94] of men, 50
That no man hath access by day to her.

VALENTINE
Why then I would resort to her by night.

---

[91] tenor – meaning or substance of something
[92] break – make a disclosure, reveal information
[93] severely – rigorously
[94] resort – visit, bring one's self to a place

DUKE
Ay, but the doors be lock'd and keys kept safe,
That no man hath recourse[95] to her by night.

VALENTINE
What lets[96] but one may enter at her window? 55

DUKE
Her chamber is aloft, far from the ground.

VALENTINE
Why then, a ladder quaintly made of cords,
To cast up, with a pair of anchoring hooks,
Would serve to scale another Hero's[97] tower.

DUKE
Now, as thou art a gentleman of blood, 60
Advise me where I may have such a ladder.
And how shall I convey the ladder thither?

VALENTINE
It will be light, my lord, that you may bear it
Under a cloak that is of any length.

DUKE
A cloak as long as thine will serve the turn? 65

VALENTINE
Ay, my good lord.

DUKE
I pray thee, let me feel thy cloak upon me.

He finds a letter in the cloak

What letter is this same? What's here? 'To Silvia'!
(*Reads*) 'Silvia, this night I will enfranchise[98] thee'.
'Tis so; and here's the ladder for the purpose. 70

---
[95] recourse – access, admission
[96] lets – hinders
[97] Hero – virgin priestess of Aphrodite, mistress to Leander. Lit a tower light as a guide for him to swim to her every evening.
[98] enfranchise – to set at liberty, to free

Go, base intruder, overweening[99] slave!
Bestow thy fawning smiles on equal mates,
And think my patience, more than thy desert,
Is privilege for thy departure hence.
But if thou linger in my territories, 75
By heaven, my wrath shall far exceed the love
I ever bore my daughter or thyself.
Be gone! I will not hear thy vain[100] excuse.

Exit

VALENTINE
And why not death rather than living torment?
To die is to be banish'd from myself, 80
And Silvia is myself. Banish'd from her
Is self from self; a deadly banishment!
What light is light, if Silvia be not seen?
What joy is joy, if Silvia be not by?
Unless I look on Silvia in the day, 85
There is no day for me to look upon.
She is my essence, and I leave to be,
If I be not by her fair influence
Foster'd, illumined, cherish'd, kept alive.
I fly not death, to fly his deadly doom. 90
Tarry[101] I here, I but attend on death,
But, fly I hence, I fly away from life.

Enter PROTEUS

PROTEUS
Valentine?

VALENTINE
No.

PROTEUS
Who then? His spirit? 95

---

[99] overweening – arrogant, presumptuous
[100] vain – empty, idle, superficial
[101] tarry – remain in a place

VALENTINE
Neither.

PROTEUS
Friend Valentine, a word.

VALENTINE
                What is your news?

PROTEUS
That thou art banished, O, that's the news! –
From hence, from Silvia and from me, thy friend.

VALENTINE
O, I have fed upon this woe already,   100
Doth Silvia know that I am banished?

PROTEUS
Ay, ay, and she hath offer'd to the doom
A sea of melting pearl, which some call tears.
Those at her father's churlish[102] feet she tender'd.[103]
But neither bended knees, pure hands held up,   105
Sad sighs, deep groans, nor silver-shedding tears,
Could penetrate her uncompassionate sire;[104]
But Valentine, if he be ta'en, must die.

VALENTINE
No more, unless the next word that thou speak'st
Have some malignant[105] power upon my life.   110

PROTEUS
Time is the nurse and breeder of all good.
Here if thou stay, thou canst not see thy love;
Besides, thy staying will abridge[106] thy life.
Come, I'll convey thee through the city-gate.

VALENTINE
O my dear Silvia! Hapless Valentine!   115

---

[102] churlish – rough, rude, brutal
[103] tender'd – offered, presented
[104] sire – father
[105] malignant – hostile, injurious
[106] abridge – shorten

Exeunt VALENTINE and PROTEUS
Enter LAUNCE

LAUNCE
I am but a fool, look you; and yet I have the wit to think my master is a kind of a knave:[107] but that's all one, if he be but one knave. He lives not now that knows me to be in love; yet I am in love; but a team of horse shall not pluck that from me; nor who 'tis I love; and yet 'tis a woman; but what woman, I will not tell myself; and yet 'tis a milkmaid; yet 'tis not a maid,[108] for she hath had gossips;[109] yet 'tis a maid, for she is her master's maid,[110] and serves for wages. She hath more qualities than a water-spaniel; she can fetch and carry; she can milk –

Pulling out a paper. Enter SPEED

SPEED
How now, Signior Launce, what news with your mastership?

LAUNCE
With my master's ship? Why, it is at sea.

SPEED
What then?

LAUNCE
Why then will I tell thee that thy master stays for thee at the North Gate.

SPEED
For me? And must I go to him?

LAUNCE
Thou must run to him, for thou hast stayed so long that going will scarce serve the turn.[111]

SPEED
Why didst not tell me sooner? Pox[112] of your love letters!

Exeunt

[107] knave – rascal, villain
[108] maid – virgin
[109] gossips – sponsors for a child of hers at baptism
[110] master's maid – female servant
[111] serve the turn – to be just the thing required to do
[112] pox – used as a slight curse, referring to smallpox

ACT III, SCENE II. The DUKE's palace.
Enter DUKE and THURIO

DUKE
Sir Thurio, fear not but that she will love you
Now Valentine is banish'd from her sight.

THURIO
Since his exile she hath despised me most,
Forsworn my company and rail'd at me.

DUKE
A little time will melt her frozen thoughts 5
And worthless Valentine shall be forgot.

Enter PROTEUS

How now, Sir Proteus! Is your countryman,
According to our proclamation, gone?

PROTEUS
Gone, my good lord.

DUKE
My daughter takes his going grievously. 10

PROTEUS
A little time, my lord, will kill that grief.

DUKE
So I believe, but Thurio thinks not so.
Thou know'st how willingly I would effect
The match between Sir Thurio and my daughter?

PROTEUS
I do, my lord. 15

DUKE
And also, I think, thou art not ignorant
How she opposes her against my will.

PROTEUS
She did, my lord, when Valentine was here.

DUKE
What might we do to make the girl forget
The love of Valentine and love Sir Thurio? 20

PROTEUS
The best way is to slander Valentine
With falsehood, cowardice and poor descent,[113]
Three things that women highly hold in hate.

DUKE
Ay, but she'll think that it is spoke in hate.

PROTEUS
Ay, if his enemy deliver it: 25
Therefore it must with circumstance be spoken
By one whom she esteemeth[114] as his friend.

DUKE
Then you must undertake to slander him.

PROTEUS
'Tis an ill office for a gentleman,
Especially against his very friend. 30
But say this weed[115] her love from Valentine,
It follows not that she will love Sir Thurio.

THURIO
Therefore, as you unwind her love from him.
You must provide to bottom it[116] on me;
Which must be done by praising me as much 35
As you in worth dispraise Sir Valentine.

DUKE
And Proteus, we dare trust you in this kind.
Upon this warrant shall you have access
Where you with Silvia may confer[117] at large.
For she is lumpish,[118] heavy, melancholy, 40
And, for your friend's sake, will be glad of you.

---

[113] descent – lineage
[114] esteemeth – values, estimates
[115] weed – to root out, to take away
[116] bottom it – to wind, to twist thread
[117] confer – to talk
[118] lumpish – dull, spiritless

PROTEUS
As much as I can do, I will effect.
But you, Sir Thurio, are not sharp enough.
You must lay lime[119] to tangle her desires;
Say that upon the altar of her beauty   45
You sacrifice your tears, your sighs, your heart.
Visit by night your lady's chamber-window
With some sweet concert; tune your instruments.
This, or else nothing, will inherit[120] her.

THURIO
And thy advice this night I'll put in practice.   50
Therefore, sweet Proteus, my direction-giver,
Let us into the city presently
To sort some gentlemen well skill'd in music.
I have a sonnet that will serve the turn
To give the onset[121] to thy good advice.   55

DUKE
About it, gentlemen!

Exeunt

ACT IV, SCENE I. The frontiers of Mantua. A forest.
Enter certain Outlaws

First Outlaw
Fellows, stand fast. I see a passenger.

Second Outlaw
If there be ten, shrink not, but down with 'em.

Enter VALENTINE and SPEED

Third Outlaw
Stand, sir, and throw us[122] that you have about ye.
If not, we'll make you sit and rifle[123] you.

---

[119] lime – sticky substance laid on twigs to catch birds
[120] inherit – possess, enjoy, obtain
[121] onset – beginning, setting about
[122] throw us – fling, cast
[123] rifle – to rob, to strip

VALENTINE
(*Aside*) These are the villains
That all the travellers do fear so much.
My friends, –

First Outlaw
That's not so, sir. We are your enemies.

Second Outlaw
Peace! we'll hear him.

Third Outlaw
Ay, by my beard, will we, for he's a proper man.

VALENTINE
Then know that I have little wealth to lose.
My riches are these poor habiliments,[124]
Of which if you should here disfurnish me,
You take the sum and substance that I have.

Second Outlaw
Whither travel you?

VALENTINE
To Verona.

Third Outlaw
Whence came you?

VALENTINE
From Milan.

Third Outlaw
Have you long sojourned[125] there?

VALENTINE
Some sixteen months, and longer might have stay'd,
If crooked fortune had not thwarted me.

First Outlaw
What, were you banish'd thence?

VALENTINE
                  I was.

---

[124] habiliments – clothes
[125] sojourned – stayed, dwelled for a time

Second Outlaw

                                          For what offence?

VALENTINE
I kill'd a man, whose death I much repent.

First Outlaw
Why, ne'er repent it, if it were done so.
But were you banish'd for so small a fault?   25

VALENTINE
I was.

Third Outlaw
By the bare scalp of Robin Hood's fat friar,
This fellow were a king for our wild faction![126]

First Outlaw
We'll have him.

Third Outlaw
Know, then, that some of us are gentlemen.   30
Myself was from Verona banished
For practising to steal away a lady,
An heir, and near allied unto the Duke.

Second Outlaw
And I from Mantua, for a gentleman,
Who, in my mood, I stabb'd unto the heart.   35

First Outlaw
And I for such like petty crimes as these,
But to the purpose.

Second Outlaw
Are you content to be our general
And live, as we do, in this wilderness?

Third Outlaw
What say'st thou? Wilt thou be of our consort?[127]   40
We'll do thee homage and be ruled by thee,
Love thee as our commander and our king.

---

[126] faction – company
[127] consort – company, fellowship

First Outlaw
But if thou scorn our courtesy, thou diest.

VALENTINE
I take your offer and will live with you,
Provided that you do no outrages
On silly women or poor passengers.

Third Outlaw
No, we detest such vile base practices.
Come, go with us, we'll bring thee to our crews
And show thee all the treasure we have got,
Which, with ourselves, all rest at thy dispose.

Exeunt

ACT IV, SCENE II. Milan. The DUKE's palace. Under SILVIA's chamber.
Enter PROTEUS

PROTEUS
Already have I been false to Valentine
And now I must be as unjust to Thurio.
Under the colour of commending him,
I have access my own love to prefer.
But Silvia is too fair, too true, too holy
To be corrupted with my worthless gifts.
When I protest true loyalty to her,
She twits[128] me with my falsehood to my friend.
When to her beauty I commend my vows,
She bids me think how I have been forsworn
In breaking faith with Julia whom I loved.

Enter THURIO

THURIO
How now, Sir Proteus, are you crept before us?

PROTEUS
Ay, gentle Thurio, for you know that love
Will creep in service where it cannot go.

---

[128] twits – reproaches with contempt, mocks with disapproval

THURIO
Ay, but I hope, sir, that you love not here. 15

PROTEUS
Sir, but I do, or else I would be hence.

THURIO
Who? Silvia?

PROTEUS
      Ay, Silvia; for your sake.

THURIO
I thank you for your own.

Enter, at a distance JULIA in boy's clothes
THURIO and PROTEUS sing

Who is Silvia? what is she,
That all our swains[129] commend her? 20
Holy, fair and wise is she.
The heaven such grace did lend her,
That she might admired be.
Is she kind as she is fair?
For beauty lives with kindness. 25

Then to Silvia let us sing,
That Silvia is excelling.
She excels each mortal thing
Upon the dull earth dwelling.
To her let us garlands bring. 30

JULIA
(*Aside*) Oh yet so false that grieves my very heart-strings.
I would I were deaf. Hark, what fine change is in the music!

PROTEUS
Sir Thurio, fear not you. I will so plead
That you shall say my cunning drift excels.

---

[129] swains – youthful lovers

THURIO
Where meet we?

PROTEUS
        At Saint Gregory's well.

THURIO
                        Farewell.   35

Exit THURIO
Enter SILVIA above. JULIA hidden

PROTEUS
Madam, good even to your ladyship.

SILVIA
I thank you for your music, gentlemen.
Who is that that spake?

PROTEUS
One, lady, if you knew his pure heart's truth,
You would quickly learn to know him by his voice.   40

SILVIA
Sir Proteus, as I take it.

PROTEUS
Sir Proteus, gentle lady, and your servant.

SILVIA
What's your will?

PROTEUS
        That I may compass yours.

SILVIA
You have your wish. My will is even this,
That presently you hie[130] you home to bed.   45
Thou subtle, perjured, false, disloyal man!
Think'st thou I am so shallow, so conceitless,[131]
To be seduced by thy flattery,
That hast deceived so many with thy vows?

---

[130] hie – make haste, leave quickly
[131] conceitless – stupid

PROTEUS
I grant, sweet love, that I did love a lady, 50
But she is dead.

JULIA
      (*Aside*) 'Twere false, if I should speak it,
For I am sure she is not buried.

SILVIA
Say that she be, yet Valentine, thy friend
Survives, to whom, thyself art witness,
I am betroth'd. And art thou not ashamed 55
To wrong him with thy importunacy?[132]

PROTEUS
I likewise hear that Valentine is dead.

SILVIA
And so suppose am I, for in his grave
Assure thyself my love is buried.

PROTEUS
Sweet lady, let me rake[133] it from the earth. 60

SILVIA
Go to thy lady's grave and call hers thence.

PROTEUS
Madam, if your heart be so obdurate,[134]
Vouchsafe[135] me yet your picture for my love.
For since the substance of your perfect self
Is else devoted, I am but a shadow, 65
And to your shadow will I make true love.

JULIA
(*Aside*) If 'twere a substance, you would sure deceive it,
And make it but a shadow, as I am.

SILVIA
I am very loath to be your idol, sir,
But since your falsehood shall become you well 70

---

[132] importunacy – urgent solicitation
[133] rake – bring to light, scrape
[134] obdurate – stubborn, hard-hearted
[135] vouchsafe – to grant, to condescend to do

To worship shadows and adore false shapes,
Send to me in the morning and I'll send it.
And so, good rest.

Exeunt PROTEUS and SILVIA severally

JULIA
Oh it hath been the longest night
That e'er I watch'd and the most heaviest. 75

Exit

ACT IV, SCENE III. The same.
Enter EGLAMOUR

EGLAMOUR
This is the hour that Madam Silvia
Entreated me to call and know her mind.
There's some great matter she'd employ me in.
Madam, madam!

Enter SILVIA above

SILVIA
                Who calls?

EGLAMOUR
                        Your servant and your friend;
One that attends your ladyship's command. 5

SILVIA
Sir Eglamour, a thousand times good morrow.

EGLAMOUR
As many, worthy lady, to yourself.
I am thus early come to know what service
It is your pleasure to command me in.

SILVIA
O Eglamour, thou art a gentleman, 10
Think not I flatter, for I swear I do not;

Valiant, wise, remorseful, well accomplish'd.
Thou art not ignorant what dear good will
I bear unto the banish'd Valentine,
Nor how my father would enforce me marry   15
Vain Thurio, whom my very soul abhors.[136]
Sir Eglamour, I would to Valentine,
To Mantua, where I hear he makes abode;[137]
And for the ways are dangerous to pass,
I do desire thy worthy company,   20
Upon whose faith and honour I repose;[138]
To bear me company and go with me.
If not, to hide what I have said to thee
That I may venture to depart alone.

EGLAMOUR
Madam, I pity much your grievances,   25
Which, since I know they virtuously are placed,
I give consent to go along with you.
When will you go?

SILVIA
                This evening coming.

EGLAMOUR
Where shall I meet you?

SILVIA
                At Friar Patrick's cell,
Where I intend holy confession.   30

EGLAMOUR
I will not fail your ladyship.
Good morrow, gentle lady.

SILVIA
Good morrow, kind Sir Eglamour.

Exeunt

[136] abhors – detests, loathes
[137] abode – to dwell, to live
[138] repose – to confide

ACT IV, SCENE IV. The same.

Enter LAUNCE, with his dog

LAUNCE
When a man's servant shall play the cur[139] with him, look you, it goes hard. One that I brought up of a puppy. I have taught him, even as one would say precisely 'Thus I would teach a dog'. I was sent to deliver him as a present to Mistress Silvia from my master, and I came no sooner into the dining-chamber but he steps me[140] to 5
her trencher[141] and steals her capon's leg.[142] O, 'tis a foul thing when a cur cannot keep him- self in all companies! If I had not had more wit than he, to take a fault upon me that he did, I think verily he had been hanged for't. You shall judge. He thrusts me himself into the company of three or four gentleman-like dogs under the 10
Duke's table. He had not been there – bless the mark! – a pissing one. while, but all the chamber smelt him. 'Out with the dog!' says 'What cur is that?' says another. 'Hang him up' says the Duke. I, having been acquainted with the smell before, knew it was Crab, and goes me to the fellow that whips the dogs: 'Friend', quoth I, 'You 15
do him the more wrong, 'twas I did the thing you wot[143] of'. He makes me no more ado, but whips me out of the chamber. How many masters would do this for his servant? When didst thou see me heave up my leg and make water[144] against a gentlewoman's farthingale?[145] Didst thou ever see me do such a trick? 20

Enter PROTEUS and JULIA, disguised

PROTEUS
Sebastian is thy name? I like thee well
And will employ thee in some service presently.

JULIA
In what you please. I'll do what I can.

---

[139] cur – term of contempt for a dog
[140] steps me – goes a little distance and with purpose
[141] trencher – plate
[142] capon's leg – chicken's leg, castrated cock fattened for eating
[143] wot – to know, used of humble persons striving for decency
[144] make water – urinate
[145] farthingale – a hoop petticoat

PROTEUS
I hope thou wilt. (*To LAUNCE*) How now, you whoreson[146]
peasant! Where have you been these two days loitering? 25

LAUNCE
Marry, sir, I carried Mistress Silvia the dog you bade me.

PROTEUS
And what says she to my little jewel?

LAUNCE
Marry, she says your dog was a cur, and tells you currish[147]
thanks is good enough for such a present.

PROTEUS
But she received my dog? 30

LAUNCE
No, indeed, did she not. Here have I brought him back again.

PROTEUS
What, didst thou offer her this from me?

LAUNCE
Ay, sir. The other squirrel[148] was stolen from me by the hangman
boys in the market-place, and then I offered her mine own.

PROTEUS
Go get thee hence, and find my dog again. 35
Away, I say!

Exit LAUNCE

Sebastian, I have entertained thee,
Partly that I have need of such a youth
That can with some discretion do my business,
For 'tis no trusting to yond foolish lout.[149] 40
Go presently and take this ring with thee,
Deliver it to Madam Silvia.
She loved me well deliver'd it to me.

---

[146] whoreson – term of reproach used in coarse tenderness
[147] currish – becoming a dog
[148] squirrel – dog, runt of the litter
[149] lout – awkward and foolish fellow

JULIA
It seems you loved not her, to leave her token.
She is dead, belike?

PROTEUS
                Not so. I think she lives.   45

JULIA
Alas!

PROTEUS
    Why dost thou cry 'Alas'?

JULIA
I cannot choose but pity her.

PROTEUS
Wherefore shouldst thou pity her?

JULIA
Because methinks that she loved you as well
As you do love your lady Silvia.   50
She dreams of him that has forgot her love;
You dote[150] on her that cares not for your love.
'Tis pity love should be so contrary,
And thinking of it makes me cry 'Alas!'

PROTEUS
Well, give her that ring and therewithal   55
This letter. That's her chamber. Tell my lady
I claim the promise for her heavenly picture.

Exit

JULIA
How many women would do such a message?
Alas, poor Proteus! Thou hast entertain'd
A fox to be the shepherd of thy lambs.   60
Alas, poor fool, why do I pity him
That with his very heart despiseth me?
Because he loves her, he despiseth me.
Because I love him I must pity him.

---

[150] dote – love to excess

This ring I gave him when he parted from me, 65
To bind him to remember my good will.
And now am I, unhappy messenger,
To plead for that which I would not obtain.
I am my master's true-confirmed love,
But cannot be true servant to my master, 70
Unless I prove false traitor to myself.
Yet will I woo for him, but yet so coldly
As, heaven it knows, I would not have him speed.[151]

Enter SILVIA

Gentlewoman, good day! I pray you, be my mean
To bring me where to speak with Madam Silvia. 75

SILVIA
What would you with her, if that I be she?

JULIA
If you be she, I do entreat your patience
To hear me speak the message I am sent on.

SILVIA
From whom?

JULIA
From my master, Sir Proteus, madam. 80

SILVIA
O, he sends you for a picture?

JULIA
Ay, madam.

SILVIA
Go, give your master this. Tell him from me,
One Julia, that his changing thoughts forget,
Would better fit his chamber than this shadow.[152] 85

JULIA
Madam, please you peruse this letter –

[151] speed – succeed
[152] shadow – picture, portrait

SILVIA
I will not look upon your master's lines.
I know they are stuff'd with protestations
And full of new-found oaths, which he will break
As easily as I do tear his paper. 90

JULIA
Madam, he sends your ladyship this ring.

SILVIA
The more shame for him that he sends it me;
For I have heard him say a thousand times
His Julia gave it him at his departure.
Though his false finger have profaned[153] the ring, 95
Mine shall not do his Julia so much wrong.

JULIA
She thanks you.

SILVIA
What say'st thou?

JULIA
I thank you, madam, that you tender her.
Poor gentlewoman, my master wrongs her much. 100

SILVIA
Dost thou know her?

JULIA
Almost as well as I do know myself.

SILVIA
Belike she thinks that Proteus hath forsook her.

JULIA
I think she doth; and that's her cause of sorrow.

SILVIA
Is she not passing fair? 105

---

[153] profaned – polluted, desecrated

JULIA
She hath been fairer, madam, than she is.
When she did think my master loved her well
She, in my judgement, was as fair as you.

SILVIA
Alas, poor lady, desolate and left!
Here youth, there is my purse. I give thee this   110
For thy sweet mistress' sake, because thou lovest her.
Farewell.

Exit SILVIA

JULIA
And she shall thank you for't, if e'er you know her.
A virtuous gentlewoman, mild and beautiful.
Here is her picture. Let me see; I think,   115
If I had such a tire,[154] this face of mine
Were full as lovely as is this of hers.
And yet the painter flatter'd her a little,
Unless I flatter with myself too much.
What should it be that he respects in her   120
But I can make respective[155] in myself,
If this fond Love were not a blinded god?
Come, shadow,[156] come and take this shadow up,
For 'tis thy rival. O thou senseless form;
I'll use thee kindly for thy mistress' sake,   125
That used me so; or else, by Jove I vow,
I should have scratch'd out your unseeing eyes
To make my master out of love with thee!

Exit

---

[154] tire – adornment
[155] respective – worthy of being cared for
[156] shadow – worthless person

ACT V, SCENE I. Milan. An abbey.

Enter EGLAMOUR

EGLAMOUR
Now it is about the very hour
That Silvia, at Friar Patrick's cell, should meet me.
She will not fail, for lovers break not hours,
Unless it be to come before their time.

Enter SILVIA

Lady, a happy evening! 5

SILVIA
Amen, amen! Go on, good Eglamour,
Out at the postern[157] by the abbey wall.
I fear I am attended by some spies.

EGLAMOUR
Fear not. The forest is not three leagues[158] off.
If we recover[159] that, we are sure[160] enough. 10

Exeunt

ACT V, SCENE II. The same. The DUKE's palace.

Enter THURIO, PROTEUS, and JULIA

THURIO
Sir Proteus, what says Silvia to my suit?[161]

PROTEUS
O sir, I find her milder than she was,
And yet she takes exceptions[162] at your person.

THURIO
What says she to my face?

---

[157] postern – small gate
[158] leagues – measure of length, about three miles
[159] recover – gain, reach
[160] sure – secure, safe
[161] suit – amorous solicitation, courtship, proposal
[162] exceptions – disapproval

PROTEUS
She says it is a fair one. 5

THURIO
How likes she my discourse?[163]

PROTEUS
Ill, when you talk of war.

THURIO
But well, when I discourse of love and peace?

JULIA
(*Aside*) But better, indeed, when you hold your peace.

THURIO
What says she to my valour? 10

PROTEUS
O sir, she makes no doubt of that.

JULIA
(*Aside*) She needs not, when she knows it cowardice.

THURIO
What says she to my birth?

PROTEUS
That you are well derived.

JULIA
(*Aside*) True; from a gentleman to a fool. 15

Enter DUKE

DUKE
How now, Sir Proteus. How now, Thurio.
Which of you saw Sir Eglamour of late?

THURIO
Not I.

PROTEUS
    Nor I.

---

[163] discourse – conversation

DUKE
        Saw you my daughter?

PROTEUS
              Neither.

DUKE
Why then, she's fled unto that peasant Valentine,
And Eglamour is in her company.   20
Therefore, I pray you, stand not to discourse,
But mount you presently and meet with me
Upon the rising of the mountain foot
That leads towards Mantua, whither they are fled.
Dispatch, sweet gentlemen, and follow me.   25

Exit

THURIO
Why, this it is to be a peevish[164] girl,
That flies her fortune when it follows her.
I'll after, more to be revenged on Eglamour
Than for the love of reckless Silvia.

Exit

PROTEUS
And I will follow, more for Silvia's love   30
Than hate of Eglamour that goes with her.

Exit

JULIA
And I will follow, more to cross that love
Than hate for Silvia that is gone for love.

Exit

---

[164] peevish – silly, childish, thoughtless

ACT V, SCENE III. The frontiers of Mantua. The forest.
Enter Outlaws with SILVIA

First Outlaw
Come, come, be patient. We must bring you to our captain.

SILVIA
A thousand more mischances than this one
Have learn'd me how to brook[165] this patiently.

First Outlaw
Where is the gentleman that was with her?

Second Outlaw
Being nimble-footed, he hath outrun us.　　　　　　　　　　　　5
Go thou with her to the west end of the wood.
There is our captain. We'll follow him that's fled;

First Outlaw
Come, I must bring you to our captain's cave.
Fear not. He bears an honourable mind,
And will not use a woman lawlessly.　　　　　　　　　　　　　10

SILVIA
O Valentine, this I endure for thee!

Exeunt

ACT V, SCENE IV. Another part of the forest.
Enter VALENTINE

VALENTINE
This shadowy desert, unfrequented woods,
I better brook than flourishing peopled towns.
Here can I sit alone, unseen of any,
And to the nightingale's complaining notes
Tune my distresses and record my woes.　　　　　　　　　　　　5
Repair me with thy presence, Silvia.
Thou gentle nymph,[166] cherish thy forlorn swain![167]

---

[165] brook – endure
[166] nymph – a beautiful woman
[167] forlorn swain – unhappy young lover

What hallooing[168] and what stir is this today?
Withdraw thee, Valentine. Who's this comes here?

VALENTINE stands aside
Enter PROTEUS, SILVIA, and JULIA

PROTEUS
Madam, this service I have done for you, 10
Though you respect not aught your servant doth,
To hazard[169] life and rescue you from him
That would have forced your honour and your love.
Vouchsafe me for my meed[170] but one fair look.

VALENTINE
(*Aside*) How like a dream is this I see and hear! 15
Love, lend me patience to forbear awhile.

SILVIA
O miserable, unhappy that I am!

PROTEUS
Unhappy were you, madam, ere I came.
But by my coming I have made you happy.

SILVIA
By thy approach thou makest me most unhappy. 20

JULIA
(*Aside*) And me, when he approacheth to your presence.

SILVIA
Had I been seized by a hungry lion,
I would have been a breakfast to the beast,
Rather than have false Proteus rescue me.
O heaven be judge how I love Valentine, 25
Whose life's as tender to me as my soul!
I do detest false perjured Proteus.
Therefore be gone, solicit me no more.

PROTEUS
O, 'tis the curse in love, and still approved,
When women cannot love where they're beloved! 30

[168] hallooing – to cry out, shouting or calling with a loud voice
[169] hazard – to risk
[170] meed – reward, recompense

SILVIA
When Proteus cannot love where he's beloved.
Read over Julia's heart, thy first best love,
For whose dear sake thou didst then rend[171] thy faith
Into a thousand oaths, and all those oaths
Descended into perjury, to love me.   35
Thou counterfeit to thy true friend!

PROTEUS
                    In love
Who respects friend?

SILVIA
                    All men but Proteus.

PROTEUS
Nay, if the gentle spirit of moving words
Can no way change you to a milder form,
I'll woo you like a soldier, at arms' end,[172]   40
And love you 'gainst the nature of love, – force ye.

SILVIA
O heaven!

PROTEUS
          I'll force thee yield to my desire.

VALENTINE
Ruffian, let go that rude uncivil touch,
Thou friend of an ill fashion!

PROTEUS
                    Valentine!

VALENTINE
Thou common[173] friend, that's without faith or love,   45
For such is a friend now. Treacherous man!
Who should be trusted, when one's own right hand
Is perjured to the bosom? Proteus,
I am sorry I must never trust thee more,
But count the world a stranger for thy sake.   50

---
[171] rend – to tear, to split
[172] arm's end – laying hands on thee as weapons instead of useless words
[173] common – vulgar

PROTEUS
My shame and guilt confounds me.
Forgive me, Valentine. If hearty sorrow
Be a sufficient ransom for offence,
I tender 't here. I do as truly suffer
As e'er I did commit.

VALENTINE
                Then I am paid; 55
And once again I do receive thee honest.
Who by repentance is not satisfied
Is nor of heaven nor earth, for these are pleased.
By penitence the Eternal's wrath's appeased.
And, that my love may appear plain and free, 60
All that was mine in Silvia I give thee.

JULIA
O me unhappy!

JULIA swoons

PROTEUS
           Look to the boy.

VALENTINE
                  Why, boy!
Why wag,[174] how now! What's the matter? Look up. Speak.

JULIA
O good sir, my master charged me to deliver a ring to Madam
Silvia, which, out of my neglect, was never done. 65

PROTEUS
Where is that ring, boy?

JULIA
Here 'tis. This is it.

She gives him the ring

PROTEUS
Why, this is the ring I gave to Julia.

---

[174] wag – silly jester, buffoon

JULIA
O, cry you mercy, sir, I have mistook.

She offers PROTEUS another ring

This is the ring you sent to Silvia. 70

PROTEUS
But how camest thou by this ring? At my depart
I gave this unto Julia.

JULIA
And Julia herself did give it me,
And Julia herself hath brought it hither.

JULIA reveals herself

PROTEUS
How? Julia? 75

JULIA
Behold her that gave aim to all thy oaths,
And entertain'd 'em deeply in her heart.
How oft hast thou with perjury cleft the root![175]
O Proteus, let this habit[176] make thee blush!
Be thou ashamed that I have took upon me 80
Such an immodest raiment,[177] if shame live
In a disguise of love.
It is the lesser blot, modesty finds,
Women to change their shapes than men their minds.

PROTEUS
Than men their minds! 'Tis true. O heaven! Were man 85
But constant, he were perfect. That one error
Fills him with faults, makes him run through all the sins;
Inconstancy falls off ere it begins.
What is in Silvia's face, but I may spy
More fresh in Julia's with a constant eye? 90

---

[175] cleft the root – broken the heart
[176] habit – dress, garb
[177] raiment – dress, clothing

VALENTINE
Come, come, a hand from either.
Let me be blest to make this happy close.[178]
'Twere pity two such friends should be long foes.

JULIA and PROTEUS join hands

PROTEUS
Bear witness, heaven, I have my wish for ever.

JULIA
And I mine. 95

Enter DUKE and THURIO

VALENTINE
Forbear, forbear, I say! It is my lord the Duke.
Your grace is welcome to a man disgraced,
Banished Valentine.

DUKE
              Sir Valentine!

THURIO
Yonder is Silvia, and Silvia's mine.

VALENTINE
Thurio, give back, or else embrace thy death. 100
Come not within the measure[179] of my wrath.
Do not name Silvia thine. If once again,
Verona shall not hold thee. Here she stands;
Take but possession of her with a touch –
I dare thee but to breathe upon my love. 105

THURIO
I hold him but a fool that will endanger
His body for a girl that loves him not.
I claim her not, and therefore she is thine.

Exit

---

[178] close – union
[179] within the measure – within the reach

DUKE
Now, by the honour of my ancestry,
I do applaud thy spirit, Valentine, 110
And think thee worthy of an empress' love.
Know then, I here forget all former griefs,
Cancel all grudge, repeal[180] thee home again,
Plead a new state[181] in thy unrivall'd merit,
To which I thus subscribe: Sir Valentine, 115
Thou art a gentleman and well derived.[182]
Take thou thy Silvia, for thou hast deserved her.

VALENTINE
I thank your grace. The gift hath made me happy.

DUKE
Come, let us go.

VALENTINE
And, as we walk along, I dare be bold 120
With our discourse to make your grace to smile.
What think you of this page, my lord?

DUKE
I think the boy hath grace in him. He blushes.

VALENTINE
I warrant you, my lord, more grace than boy.

DUKE
What mean you by that saying? 125

VALENTINE
Please you, I'll tell you as we pass along,
That you will wonder what hath fortuned.[183]
Come, Proteus, 'tis your penance but to hear
The story of your loves discovered.
That done, our day of marriage shall be yours, 130
One feast, one house, one mutual happiness.

Exeunt

---

[180] repeal – recall from exile
[181] plead a new state – give support for something
[182] derived – descended
[183] fortuned – happened, come to pass

8
TWO GENTLEMEN OF VERONA

Suggested cast list and character assignments for a small cast

<u>6 actors, gender flexible. Cast can also be as large as 13 actors.</u>

　　Actor 1 – Valentine, Eglamor
　　Actor 2 – Proteus, Second Outlaw
　　Actor 3 – Julia, First Outlaw
　　Actor 4 – Sylvia, Third Outlaw
　　Actor 5 – Lucetta, Speed, Thurio
　　Actor 6 – Duke, Launce

9
THE TEMPEST

William Shakespeare

Originally written – 1610–1611
First Published – 1623
First recorded performance – 1611

Edited and Abridged by Julie Fain Lawrence-Edsell
(adapted from http://shakespeare.mit.edu)

Dramatis Personae

ALONSO, King of Naples
SEBASTIAN, his brother
PROSPERO, the right Duke of Milan
ANTONIO, his brother, the usurping Duke of Milan
FERDINAND, son to the King of Naples
GONZALO, an honest Old Councellor
CALIBAN, a savage slave
TRINCULO, a jester
STEPHANO, a drunker butler
Mariners on the ship

MIRANDA, daughter of Prospero

ARIEL, an airy spirit
other spirits

ACT I, SCENE I. On a ship at sea.
A tempestuous noise of thunder and lightning heard

ARIEL
Down with the topmast! yare![1] Lower, lower!

MARINERS
We run ourselves aground![2]

ARIEL & MARINERS
A plague upon this howling!

MARINERS
All lost! to prayers, to prayers! all lost! Mercy on us!

GONZALO
Let's all sink with the King.   5

ANTONIO
Let's take leave of him.

FERDINAND
Hell is empty, and all the devils are here!

MARINERS
Mercy on us! We split, we split, we split!

Exeunt

ACT I, SCENE II. The island. Before PROSPERO's cell.
Enter PROSPERO and MIRANDA

MIRANDA
If by your art, my dearest father, you have
Put the wild waters in this roar, allay[3] them.
The sky, it seems, would pour down stinking pitch,[4]
But that the sea, mounting to the welkin's cheek,[5]
Dashes the fire out. O, I have suffered   5
With those that I saw suffer: a brave vessel,

---
[1] yare – ready, active, brisk
[2] aground – stranded, on the ground
[3] allay – mitigate, appease, abate
[4] stinking pitch – thick black substance with an offensive smell
[5] welkin's cheek – sky's clouds

Who had, no doubt, some noble creature in her,
Dash'd all to pieces. O, the cry did knock[6]
Against my very heart. Poor souls, they perish'd.

PROSPERO
No more amazement: tell your piteous heart   10
There's no harm done.

MIRANDA
                O, woe the day!

PROSPERO
                        No harm.
I have done nothing but in care of thee,
Of thee, my dear one, thee, my daughter, who
Art ignorant of what thou art, nought knowing
Of whence I am, nor that I am more better   15
Than Prospero, master of a full poor cell,[7]
And thy no greater father.

MIRANDA
                    More to know
Did never meddle with my thoughts.

PROSPERO
                          'Tis time
I should inform thee farther. Lend thy hand,
And pluck my magic garment from me. So: 20
(*Lays down his mantle*)
Lie there, my art. Wipe thou thine eyes; have comfort.
The direful spectacle of the wreck, which touch'd
The very virtue of compassion in thee,
I have with such provision in mine art
So safely ordered that there is no soul –   25
Which thou heard'st cry, which thou saw'st sink.
Obey and be attentive. Canst thou remember
A time before we came unto this cell?
I do not think thou canst, for then thou wast not
Out three years old.

---

[6] knock – beat, strike
[7] cell – small and close habitation

MIRANDA
                    Certainly, sir, I can.   30
'Tis far off and rather like a dream
Than an assurance.[8]

PROSPERO
                    Miranda, twelve year since,
Thy father was the Duke of Milan and
A prince of power.

MIRANDA
                    Sir, are not you my father?

PROSPERO
Thy mother was a piece of virtue, and   35
She said thou wast my daughter; and thy father
Was Duke of Milan; and thou his only heir
And princess no worse issued.

MIRANDA
                    O the heavens!
What foul play had we that we came from thence?

PROSPERO
My brother and thy uncle, call'd Antonio –   40
Whom next thyself of all the world I loved –
The government I cast upon[9] my brother
And to my state grew stranger,[10] being transported[11]
And rapt in secret studies. Thy false uncle –
Dost thou attend me?

MIRANDA
                    Sir, most heedfully.   45

PROSPERO
I, thus neglecting worldly ends, all dedicated
To closeness and the bettering of my mind
In my false brother –

---

[8] assurance – certain knowledge
[9] cast upon – to bestow, to impart
[10] stranger – unknown
[11] transported – to bear away the soul in ecstasy, to ravish

Awaked an evil nature; and my trust,
Like a good parent, did beget of him 50
A falsehood in its contrary as great
As my trust was. Hence his ambition growing, –
Dost thou hear?

MIRANDA
                Your tale, sir, would cure deafness.

PROSPERO
He did believe he was indeed the duke!
The King of Naples, being an enemy 55
To me inveterate,[12] hearkens[13] my brother's suit;[14]
Should presently extirpate[15] me and mine
Out of the dukedom and confer fair Milan
With all the honours on my brother: whereon,
Did Antonio open the gates of Milan, 60
And, i' the dead of darkness, hurried thence
Me and thy crying self.

MIRANDA
                Alack, for pity!
I, not remembering how I cried out then,
Will cry it o'er again.

PROSPERO
                Hear a little further,
And then I'll bring thee to the present business 65
Which now's upon's; without the which this story
Were most impertinent.
In few, they hurried us aboard a bark,[16]
Bore us some leagues[17] to sea; a bark not rigg'd,
Nor tackle, sail, nor mast; and there they hoist[18] us, 70
To cry to th' sea that roar'd.

---

[12] inveterate – of long standing, deep-rooted
[13] hearkens – listens to
[14] suit – petition
[15] extirpate – remove completely
[16] bark – ship
[17] leagues – measure of about three miles in length
[18] hoist – carried off, heaved away

MIRANDA
                    Alack, what trouble
Was I then to you!

PROSPERO
                    O, a cherubim[19]
Thou wast that did preserve me.

MIRANDA
                    How came we ashore?

PROSPERO
By Providence divine.
Some food we had and some fresh water that   75
A noble man, Gonzalo, did give us,
With garments, linens, and necessities
Which since have steaded[20] much; so, of his heart,
Knowing I loved my books, he furnish'd me
From mine own library with volumes that   80
I prize above my dukedom.
Here in this island we arrived; and here
Have I, thy schoolmaster, made thee more profit
Than other princesses can that have more time
For vainer hours and tutors not so careful.   85

MIRANDA
Heavens thank you for't! And now, I pray you, sir,
For still 'tis beating in my mind, your reason
For raising this sea-storm?

PROSPERO
                    Know thus far forth.
By accident most strange, bountiful Fortune,
Hath mine enemies brought to this shore.
Here cease more questions: 90
Thou art inclined to sleep; 'tis a good dulness,[21]
And give it way: I know thou canst not choose.

MIRANDA sleeps

---

[19] cherubim – celestial spirit
[20] steaded – helped, benefited
[21] dulness – drowsiness

Come away, servant, come. I am ready now.
Approach, my Ariel, come.

Enter ARIEL

ARIEL
All hail, great master! grave sir, hail! I come   95
To answer thy best pleasure; be't to fly,
To swim, to dive into the fire, to ride
On the curl'd clouds, to thy strong bidding task
Ariel and all his quality.

PROSPERO
                    Hast thou, spirit,
Perform'd to point the tempest that I bade thee?   100

ARIEL
To every article.
I boarded the king's ship; now on the beak,[22]
Now in the waist,[23] the deck, in every cabin,
I flamed amazement:[24] sometime I'd divide,
And burn in many places; on the topmast   105
The yards[25] and bowsprit,[26] would I flame distinctly
Then meet and join. Jove's lightenings, the cracks
Of sulphurous roaring, the most mighty Neptune
Seem to besiege and make his bold waves tremble,
Yea, his dread trident shake.

PROSPERO
                    My brave spirit!   110
Who was so firm, so constant, that this coil[27]
Would not infect his reason?

---

[22] beak – forward part of a ship below the deck
[23] waist – middle part of a ship
[24] flamed amazement – caused amazement by appearing in the form of flames
[25] yards – piece of timber used to extend a sail
[26] bowsprit – a large boom extending forward from a ship's bow
[27] coil – turmoil, confusion

ARIEL
                    Not a soul
But felt a fever of the mad and play'd
Some tricks of desperation. All but mariners
Plunged in the foaming brine[28] and quit the vessel,   115
Then all afire with me: the King's son, Ferdinand,
With hair up-staring, – then like reeds, not hair, –
Was the first man that leap'd; cried, 'Hell is empty
And all the devils are here'.

PROSPERO
                    Why that's my spirit!
But was not this nigh[29] shore?
ARIEL
                    Close by, my master.   120

PROSPERO
But are they, Ariel, safe?

ARIEL
                    Not a hair perish'd;
In troops I have dispersed them 'bout the isle.
The King's son have I landed by himself;
Whom I left cooling of the air with sighs
His arms in this sad knot.

PROSPERO
                    Of the King's ship   125
The mariners say how thou hast disposed
And all the rest o' the fleet.

ARIEL
                    Safely in harbour
Is the King's ship; in the deep nook, where once
Thou call'dst me up at midnight to fetch dew
From the still-vex'd Bermoothes,[30] there she's hid: 130
The mariners all under hatches stow'd;

---

[28] brine – sea
[29] nigh – near
[30] Bermoothes – Bermuda Islands

I have left asleep; and for the rest o' the fleet
All are upon the Mediterranean flote,[31]
Bound sadly home for Naples,
Supposing that they saw the King's ship wreck'd   135
And his great person perish.

PROSPERO
                      Ariel, thy charge[32]
Exactly is perform'd: but there's more work.

ARIEL
Is there more toil? Since thou dost give me pains,
Let me remember thee what thou hast promised,
Which is not yet perform'd me.

PROSPERO
                    How now? moody?   140
What is't thou canst demand?

ARIEL
                      My liberty.

PROSPERO
Before the time be out? no more!

ARIEL
                      I prithee,
Remember I have done thee worthy service;
Told thee no lies, made thee no mistakings, served
Without or grudge or grumblings: thou didst promise   145
To bate[33] me a full year.

PROSPERO
                  Dost thou forget
From what a torment I did free thee?

ARIEL
                      No.

PROSPERO
Thou dost, and think'st it much –

---

[31] flote – flood, sea
[32] charge – order, commission
[33] bate – refrain from exacting a debt

ARIEL
                              I do not, sir.

PROSPERO
Thou liest, malignant[34] thing! Hast thou forgot
The foul witch Sycorax,[35] who with age and envy   150
Was grown into a hoop?[36] Hast thou forgot her?

ARIEL
No, sir.

PROSPERO
Thou hast. Where was she born? speak; tell me.

ARIEL
Sir, in Argier.

PROSPERO
            O, was she so? I must
Once in a month recount what thou hast been,   155
Which thou forget'st. This damn'd witch Sycorax,
For mischiefs manifold and sorceries terrible
To enter human hearing, from Argier,
Thou know'st, was banish'd: for one thing she did
They would not take her life. Is not this true?   160

ARIEL
Ay, sir.

PROSPERO
This blue-eyed hag was hither brought with child
And here was left by the sailors. Thou, my slave,
As thou report'st thyself, wast then her servant;
Refusing her grand hests,[37] she did confine thee,   165
Into a cloven[38] pine; within which rift[39]
Imprison'd thou didst painfully remain
A dozen years; within which space she died
And left thee there; where thou didst vent[40] thy groans

---

[34] malignant – spiteful, malicious
[35] Sycorax – Caliban's mother
[36] hoop – circular band of wood
[37] hests – commands
[38] cloven – split, divided, cleft
[39] rift – fissure, crack
[40] vent – utter

As fast as mill-wheels strike. Then was this island – 170
Save for the son that she did litter here,
A freckled whelp[41] hag-born – not honour'd with
A human shape.

ARIEL
                Yes, Caliban her son.

PROSPERO
Dull thing, I say so; he, that Caliban
Whom now I keep in service. Thou best know'st 175
What torment I did find thee in; thy groans
Did make wolves howl and penetrate the breasts
Of ever angry bears: it was mine art,
When I arrived and heard thee, that made gape[42]
The pine and let thee out.

ARIEL
                   I thank thee, master. 180

PROSPERO
If thou more murmur'st, I will rend[43] an oak
And peg thee in his knotty entrails till
Thou hast howl'd away twelve winters.

ARIEL
                        Pardon, master;
I will be correspondent[44] to command
And do my spiriting gently.

PROSPERO
                Do so, and after two days 185
I will discharge thee.

ARIEL
             That's my noble master!
What shall I do? say what; what shall I do?

PROSPERO
Go make thyself like a nymph o' the sea: be subject
To no sight but thine and mine, invisible

---

[41] whelp – child of savage and ferocious parents
[42] gape – open wide
[43] rend – split
[44] correspondent – agreeing

To every eyeball else. Go, hence with diligence! 190

ARIEL
My lord it shall be done.

Exit ARIEL

PROSPERO
Awake, dear heart, awake! thou hast slept well;
Awake!

MIRANDA
    The strangeness[45] of your story put
Heaviness in me.

PROSPERO
        Shake it off. Come on;
We'll visit Caliban my slave, who never 195
Yields us kind answer.

MIRANDA
        'Tis a villain, sir,
I do not love to look on.

PROSPERO
        But, as 'tis,
We cannot miss him: he does make our fire,
Fetch in our wood and serves in offices
That profit us. What, ho! slave! Caliban! 200
Thou earth, thou! speak.

CALIBAN
    (*Within*) There's wood enough within.

PROSPERO
Come forth, I say! there's other business for thee:
Thou poisonous slave, got by the devil himself
Upon thy wicked dam,[46] come forth!

Enter CALIBAN

---

[45] strangeness – wonderfulness, exciting surprise
[46] dam – term of contempt for a mother

CALIBAN
As wicked dew as e'er my mother brush'd 205
With raven's feather from unwholesome fen[47]
Drop on you both! a south-west blow on ye
And blister you all o'er!

PROSPERO
For this, be sure, tonight thou shalt have cramps,
Side-stitches that shall pen thy breath up;[48] urchins[49] 210
As thick as honeycomb, each pinch more stinging
Than bees that made 'em.

CALIBAN
                I must eat my dinner.
This island's mine, by Sycorax my mother,
Which thou takest from me. When thou camest first,
Thou strokedst me and madest much of me, wouldst give me 215
Water with berries in't, and teach me how
To name the bigger light,[50] and how the less,
That burn by day and night: and then I loved thee
And show'd thee all the qualities o' the isle,
The fresh springs, brine-pits, barren place and fertile: 220
Cursed be I that did so! All the charms
Of Sycorax, toads, beetles, bats, light on you!
For I am all the subjects that you have,
Which first was mine own King: and here you sty[51] me
In this hard rock, whiles you do keep from me 225
The rest o' the island.

PROSPERO
                Thou most lying slave,
Whom stripes[52] may move, not kindness! I have used thee,
Filth as thou art, with human care, and lodged thee
In mine own cell, till thou didst seek to violate
The honour of my child. 230

---

[47] fen – bog
[48] pen thy breath up – constrain breath and make gasp
[49] urchins – hedgehogs
[50] bigger light – the sun and stars
[51] sty – lodge
[52] stripes – strokes made with a whip or stick

CALIBAN
O ho, O ho! Would't had been done!
Thou didst prevent me; I had peopled else
This isle with Calibans.

MIRANDA
                          Abhorred slave,
Which any print of goodness wilt not take,
Being capable of all ill! I pitied thee,   235
Took pains to make thee speak, taught thee each hour
One thing or other: when thou didst not, savage,
Know thine own meaning, but wouldst gabble[53] like
A thing most brutish, I endow'd thy purposes
With words that made them known. But thy vile race,   240
Though thou didst learn, had that in't which good natures
Could not abide to be with; therefore wast thou
Deservedly confined into this rock,
Who hadst deserved more than a prison.

CALIBAN
You taught me language; and my profit on't   245
Is, I know how to curse. The red plague[54] rid you
For learning me your language!

PROSPERO
                          Hag-seed,[55] hence!
Fetch us in fuel; and be quick, thou'rt best,
To answer other business. Shrug'st thou, malice?[56]
If thou neglect'st or dost unwillingly   250
What I command, I'll rack thee with old cramps,
Fill all thy bones with aches, make thee roar
That beasts shall tremble at thy din.[57]

CALIBAN
                          No, pray thee.
(*Aside*) I must obey: his art is of such power –

---

[53] gabble – utter inarticulate sounds
[54] red plague – fatal epidemic disease: used as a curse
[55] hag-seed – offspring of a wicked woman or a hag
[56] malice – inclination to harm others
[57] din – loud noise

PROSPERO
So, slave; hence! 255

Exit CALIBAN
Re-enter ARIEL, invisible, playing and singing; FERDINAND following

ARIEL
(*Sings*)
Come unto these yellow sands,
And then take hands:
Foot it featly here and there;
And, sweet sprites, the burthen[58] bear.
Hark, hark! 260
The watch-dogs bark!
(*Choral refrain*) – '*Bow-wow*'
Hark, hark! I hear
The strain of strutting chanticleer
Cry, Cock-a-diddle-dow. 265

FERDINAND
Where should this music be? I' the air or the earth?
It sounds no more: and sure, it waits upon
Some god o' the island. Sitting on a bank,
Weeping again the King my father's wreck,
This music crept by me upon the waters, 270
Allaying both their fury and my passion
With its sweet air: thence I have follow'd it,
Or it hath drawn me rather. But 'tis gone.
No, it begins again.

ARIEL
(*Sings*)
Full fathom[59] five thy father lies; 275
Of his bones are coral made;
Those are pearls that were his eyes:
Nothing of him that doth fade
But doth suffer a sea-change

---

[58] burthen – the chorus, refrain or undersong
[59] fathom – length of six feet, used to measure depth

Into something rich and strange. 280
Sea-nymphs hourly ring his knell[60]
(Choral refrain) – 'Ding-dong'
Hark! now I hear them, – Ding-dong, bell.

FERDINAND
The ditty[61] does remember my drown'd father.
This is no mortal business, nor no sound 285
That the earth owes.[62] I hear it now above me.

PROSPERO
The fringed curtains of thine eye advance
And say what thou seest yond.

MIRANDA
                  What is't? A spirit?
Lord, how it looks about! Believe me, sir,
It carries a brave form. But 'tis a spirit. 290

PROSPERO
No, wench;[63] it eats and sleeps and hath such senses
As we have, such. This gallant which thou seest
Was in the wrack;[64] he hath lost his fellows
And strays about to find 'em.

MIRANDA
                I might call him
A thing divine, for nothing natural 295
I ever saw so noble.

PROSPERO
        (*Aside*) It goes on, I see,
As my soul prompts it. Spirit, fine spirit! I'll free thee
Within two days for this.

FERDINAND
             Most sure, the goddess
On whom these airs attend! Vouchsafe[65] my prayer

---

[60] knell – sound of a bell rung at a funeral
[61] ditty – song
[62] owes – possesses, owns
[63] wench – familiar expression for a female person, used in tenderness and contempt
[64] wrack – shipwreck
[65] vouchsafe – grant, allow

May know if you remain upon this island; 300
And that you will some good instruction give
How I may bear[66] me here: my prime request,
Which I do last pronounce, is, O you wonder!
If you be maid or no?

MIRANDA
                No wonder, sir;
But certainly a maid.

FERDINAND
                My language! heavens! 305
I am the best of them that speak this speech,
Were I but where 'tis spoken.

PROSPERO
                How? the best?
What wert thou, if the King of Naples heard thee?

FERDINAND
A single thing, as I am now, that wonders
To hear thee speak of Naples. Myself am Naples, 310
Who with mine eyes, never since at ebb,[67] beheld
The King my father wrack'd.

MIRANDA
                Alack, for mercy!

FERDINAND
Yes, faith, and all his lords; the Duke of Milan
And his brave son being twain.[68]

PROSPERO
                (*Aside*) The Duke of Milan
And his more braver daughter could control thee, 315
If now 'twere fit to do't. At the first sight
They have changed eyes.[69] Delicate Ariel,
I'll set thee free for this. (*To* FERDINAND) A word, good sir;
I fear you have done yourself some wrong: a word.

---

[66] bear – behave
[67] ebb – flow of the tide
[68] twain – two
[69] changed eyes – exchanged looks

MIRANDA
Why speaks my father so ungently? This 320
Is the third man that e'er I saw, the first
That e'er I sigh'd for: pity move my father
To be inclined my way!

FERDINAND
                    O, if a virgin,
And your affection not gone forth, I'll make you
The queen of Naples.

PROSPERO
                    Soft, sir! one word more. 325
(*Aside*) They are both in either's powers; but this swift
    business
I must uneasy make, lest too light winning
Make the prize light. (*To* FERDINAND) Thou dost
    here usurp
The name thou owest not; and hast put thyself
Upon this island as a spy, to win it 330
From me, the lord on't.

FERDINAND
                    No, as I am a man.

MIRANDA
There's nothing ill can dwell in such a temple:
If the ill spirit have so fair a house,
Good things will strive to dwell with't.

PROSPERO
Speak not you for him; he's a traitor. Come.

FERDINAND
                            No; 335
I will resist such entertainment till
Mine enemy has more power.

He draws his sword, and is charmed from moving

MIRANDA
                    O dear father,
Make not too rash a trial of him, for
He's gentle and not fearful.

PROSPERO
                    What? I say,
My foot[70] my tutor? Put thy sword up, traitor;   340
For I can here disarm thee with this stick
And make thy weapon drop.

MIRANDA
                    Beseech you, father.

PROSPERO
Hence! Hang not on my garments.

MIRANDA
                    Sir, have pity;
I'll be his surety.

PROSPERO
            Silence! Not one word more!
An advocate for an imposter! Hush!   345
Thou think'st there is no more such shapes as he,
Having seen but him and Caliban: foolish wench!
To the most of men this is a Caliban
And they to him are angels.

MIRANDA
                    My affections
Are then most humble; I have no ambition   350
To see a goodlier man.

PROSPERO
                    Come on; obey:
Thy nerves are in their infancy again
And have no vigour in them.

FERDINAND
                    So they are;
My spirits, as in a dream, are all bound up.[71]
My father's loss, the weakness which I feel,   355
The wreck of all my friends, nor this man's threats,
To whom I am subdued, are but light to me,

---

[70] foot – inferior part of body
[71] bound up – paralyzed, restrained

Might I but through my prison once a day
Behold this maid.

PROSPERO

    (*To ARIEL*) Thou hast done well, fine Ariel!
(*To FERDINAND*) Follow me.

MIRANDA

                          Be of comfort;   360
My father's of a better nature, sir,
Than he appears by speech.

PROSPERO

              (*To ARIEL*) Thou shalt be free
As mountain winds: but then exactly do
All points of my command.

ARIEL

                   To the syllable.

PROSPERO

(*To MIRANDA*) Come, follow. Speak not for him.   365

Exeunt

ACT II, SCENE I. Another part of the island.

Enter ALONSO, SEBASTIAN, ANTONIO and GONZALO

GONZALO

Beseech you, sir, be merry; you have cause,
So have we all, of joy; for our escape
Is much beyond our loss.

ALONSO

                 Prithee, peace.

SEBASTIAN

He receives comfort like cold porridge.

GONZALO

Well, I have done: but yet, –   5

SEBASTIAN

He will be talking.

GONZALO

Here is everything advantageous to life.

ANTONIO
True; save means to live.

GONZALO
How lush and lusty the grass looks! how green!

ANTONIO
The ground indeed is tawny.[72] 10

GONZALO
But the rarity of it is, – which is indeed almost beyond credit, –

SEBASTIAN
As many vouched rarities are.

GONZALO
Methinks our garments are now as fresh as when we put them
on first in Afric, at the marriage of the King's fair daughter
Claribel to the King of Tunis. 15

SEBASTIAN
'Twas a sweet marriage, and we prosper well in our return.

GONZALO
Is not, sir, my doublet as fresh as the first day I wore it? I
mean, when I wore it at your daughter's marriage?

ALONSO
You cram these words into mine ears against
The stomach[73] of my sense. Would I had never 20
Married my daughter there! for, coming thence,
My son is lost and, in my rate, she too,
Who is so far from Italy removed
I ne'er again shall see her. O thou mine heir
Of Naples and of Milan, what strange fish 25
Hath made his meal on thee?

GONZALO
                    Sir, he may live:
I saw him beat the surges under him,
And ride upon their backs; he trod the water,

---

[72] tawny – yellowish-dark color
[73] stomach – inclination, disposition

Himself with his good arms in lusty stroke[74]
I not doubt he came alive to land.

ALONSO
No, no, he's gone.

SEBASTIAN
              We have lost your son,
I fear, for ever: Milan and Naples have
More widows in them of this business' making
Than we bring men to comfort them.

GONZALO
My lord Sebastian,
The truth you speak doth lack some gentleness
And time to speak it in —

SEBASTIAN
              Very well.

GONZALO
It is foul weather in us all, good sir,
When you are cloudy.

SEBASTIAN
              Foul weather?

ANTONIO
              Very foul.

GONZALO
Had I plantation[75] of this isle, my lord, —
And were the King on't, what would I do?

SEBASTIAN
'Scape being drunk for want of wine.

GONZALO
I would with such perfection govern, sir,
To excel the golden age.

SEBASTIAN
              God save his majesty!

---

[74] lusty stroke — vigorous swimming
[75] plantation — first establishment, first founding of laws

ANTONIO
Long live Gonzalo! 45

ALONSO
Prithee, no more: thou dost talk nothing to me.

GONZALO
I do well believe your highness; and did it to minister occasion
to these gentlemen, who are of such sensible and nimble lungs
that they always use to laugh at nothing.

ANTONIO
'Twas you we laughed at. 50

Enter ARIEL, invisible, playing solemn music

GONZALO
Will you laugh me asleep, for I am very heavy?

All sleep except ALONSO, SEBASTIAN, and ANTONIO

ALONSO
What, all so soon asleep! I wish mine eyes
Would, with themselves, shut up my thoughts: I find
They are inclined to do so.

ANTONIO
                    We two, my lord,
Will guard your person while you take your rest, 55
And watch your safety.

ALONSO
                    Thank you – Wondrous heavy.

ALONSO sleeps
Exit ARIEL

SEBASTIAN
What a strange drowsiness possesses them!

ANTONIO
It is the quality o' the climate.

SEBASTIAN
                    Why
Doth it not then our eyelids sink? I find not
Myself disposed to sleep.

ANTONIO
                    Nor I; my spirits are nimble.[76]
They dropp'd, as by a thunder-stroke. What might,
Worthy Sebastian? O, what might? – No more: –
My strong imagination sees a crown
Dropping upon thy head.

SEBASTIAN
                    What is it thou dids't say?

ANTONIO
Although this lord of weak remembrance,[77] this,
Professes to persuade – the King his son's alive,
'Tis as impossible that he's undrown'd
And he that sleeps here swims.

SEBASTIAN
                    I have no hope
That he's undrown'd.

ANTONIO
                    O, out of that, then, tell me,
Who's the next heir of Naples?

SEBASTIAN
                    Claribel.

ANTONIO
She that is Queen of Tunis.

SEBASTIAN
'Tis true, my brother's daughter's Queen of Tunis;
So is she heir of Naples; 'twixt which regions
There is some space.

ANTONIO
                    A space whose every cubit[78]
Seems to cry out, 'How shall that Claribel

---

[76] nimble – lively in motion
[77] weak remembrance – feeble of mind, lacking in understanding
[78] cubit – measure of eighteen inches

Measure us[79] back to Naples? Keep in Tunis,
And let Sebastian wake'.[80] Do you understand me?

SEBASTIAN
Methinks I do.

ANTONIO
                And how does your content
Tender[81] your own good fortune?

SEBASTIAN
                        I remember
You did supplant your brother Prospero.

ANTONIO
                              True: 80
And look how well my garments sit upon me.

SEBASTIAN
But, for your conscience?

ANTONIO
                    I feel not
This deity[82] in my bosom. Here lies your brother,
No better than the earth he lies upon,
If he were that which now he's like, that's dead;   85
Whom I, with this obedient steel, three inches of it,
Can lay to bed for ever –

SEBASTIAN
                     And as thou got'st Milan,
I'll come by Naples. Draw thy sword: one stroke
Shall free thee from the tribute which thou payest;
And I the King shall love thee.

ANTONIO
                        Draw together;   90
And when I rear[83] my hand, do you the like,
To fall it on Gonzalo.

---

[79] measure us – pass over
[80] wake – not to sleep
[81] tender – regard or treat with kindness
[82] deity – Godhead, divine in nature
[83] rear – raise

SEBASTIAN

                O, but one word.

They talk apart
Re-enter ARIEL, invisible

ARIEL
My master through his art foresees the danger
That you, his friend, are in; and sends me forth –
For else his project dies – to keep them living.   95
(*Sings in GONZALO's ear*)
While you here do snoring lie,
Open-eyed conspiracy
His time doth take.
If of life you keep a care,
Shake off slumber, and beware: 100
Awake, awake!

ANTONIO
Then let us both be sudden.

GONZALO

             (*Waking*) Now, good angels
Preserve the King.

The others wake

ALONSO
Why, how now? ho, awake! Why are you drawn?
Wherefore this ghastly looking?

GONZALO

                      What's the matter?   105

SEBASTIAN
Whiles we stood here securing your repose,[84]
Even now, we heard a hollow burst of bellowing
Like bulls, or rather lions: did't not wake you?

ALONSO
I heard nothing. Heard you this, Gonzalo?

---

[84] securing your repose – guarding your rest

GONZALO
Upon mine honour, sir, I heard a humming, 110
And that a strange one too, which did awake me:
I shaked you, sir, and cried: as mine eyes open'd,
I saw their weapons drawn: there was a noise,
That's verily. 'Tis best we stand upon our guard,
Or that we quit this place; let's draw our weapons. 115

ALONSO
Lead off this ground; and let's make further search
For my poor son.

GONZALO
         Heavens keep him from these beasts!
For he is, sure, i' the island.

ALONSO
         Lead away.

ARIEL
Prospero my lord shall know what I have done:
So, King, go safely on to seek thy son. 120

Exeunt

ACT II, SCENE II. Another part of the island.

Enter CALIBAN with a burden of wood. A noise of thunder heard

CALIBAN
All the infections that the sun sucks up
From bogs, fens,[85] flats, on Prosper fall and make him
By inch-meal[86] a disease! His spirits hear me
And yet I needs must curse. But they'll nor pinch,
Fright me with urchin-shows,[87] pitch me i' the mire,[88] 5
Nor lead me, like a firebrand,[89] in the dark
Out of my way, unless he bid 'em; but
For every trifle are they set upon me;

---

[85] fens – bogs
[86] inch-meal – entirely, every inch
[87] urchin-shows – the sight of hedgehogs or goblins
[88] mire – mud
[89] firebrand – a burning piece of wood

Sometime like apes that mow[90] and chatter at me
And after bite me, then like hedgehogs which   10
Lie tumbling in my barefoot way and mount
Their pricks at my footfall; sometime am I
All wound with adders[91] who with cloven[92] tongues
Do hiss me into madness.

Enter TRINCULO

                    Lo, now, lo!
Here comes a spirit of his, and to torment me   15
For bringing wood in slowly. I'll fall flat;
Perchance he will not mind me.

TRINCULO
Here's neither bush nor shrub, to bear off[93] any weather at all,
and another storm brewing; I hear it sing i' the wind: yond
same black cloud, yond huge one, looks like a foul bombard[94] that   20
would shed his liquor. If it should thunder as it did before, I
know not where to hide my head: yond same cloud cannot choose
but fall by pailfuls. What have we here? a man or a fish? dead or
alive? A fish: he smells like a fish; a very ancient and fish-like
smell. A strange fish! Legged like a man and his fins like arms!   25
Warm o' my troth! I do now let loose my opinion; this is no
fish, but an islander, that hath lately suffered by a thunderbolt.
(*Thunder*) Alas, the storm is come again! my best way is to
creep under his gaberdine;[95] there is no other shelter
hereabouts: misery acquaints a man with strange bed-fellows.   30
I will here shroud till the dregs[96] of the storm be past.

Enter STEPHANO, singing: a bottle in his hand

STEPHANO
I shall no more to sea, to sea,
Here shall I die ashore —

---

[90] mow – make faces
[91] adders – venomous snakes
[92] cloven – split
[93] bear off – to keep off, to go through
[94] bombard – large leather vessel to carry liquors
[95] gaberdine – long and loose outer garment
[96] dregs – the last residue

This is a very scurvy[97] tune to sing at a man's funeral:
(*drinks*) well, here's my comfort. 35

CALIBAN
Do not torment me: Oh!

STEPHANO
What's the matter? Have we devils here? I have not scaped
drowning to be afeard now of your four legs.

CALIBAN
The spirit torments me; Oh!

STEPHANO
This is some monster of the isle with four legs, who hath got 40
an ague.[98] Where the devil should he learn our language?

CALIBAN
Do not torment me, prithee; I'll bring my wood home faster.

STEPHANO
He's in his fit now and does not talk after the wisest. He shall
taste of my bottle. Come on your ways; open your mouth, here
is that which will give language to you, cat: open your mouth. 45

TRINCULO
I should know that voice: it should be – but he is drowned; and
these are devils: O defend me!

STEPHANO
Four legs and two voices: a most delicate monster! His forward
voice now is to speak well of his friend; his backward voice is to
utter foul speeches and to detract. 50

TRINCULO
Stephano!

STEPHANO
Doth thy other mouth call me? Mercy, mercy! This is a devil,
and no Monster.

TRINCULO
Stephano! If thou beest Stephano, touch me and speak to me.

[97] scurvy – scabby, vile
[98] ague – cold fits of fever

STEPHANO
If thou beest Trinculo, come forth. Thou art very Trinculo 55
indeed! How camest thou to be the siege[99] of this moon-calf?[100]

TRINCULO
I hid me under the dead moon-calf's gaberdine for fear of
the storm. And art thou living, Stephano?

CALIBAN
(*Aside*) That's a brave god and bears celestial liquor: I will
kneel to him. 60

STEPHANO
How didst thou 'scape? swear by this bottle how thou camest
hither. I escaped upon a butt of sack[101] which the sailors
heaved o'erboard.

CALIBAN
I'll swear upon that bottle to be thy true subject.

TRINCULO
Swum ashore, man, like a duck. O Stephano, hast any more 65
of this?

STEPHANO
The whole butt, man: my cellar is in a rock by the sea-side
where my wine is hid. How now, moon-calf!

CALIBAN
Hast thou not dropp'd from heaven?

STEPHANO
Out o' the moon, I do assure thee: I was the man i' the moon 70
when time was.

CALIBAN
I have seen thee in her and I do adore thee:
I'll show thee every fertile inch o' th' island;
I will kiss thy foot: I prithee, be my god.
I'll show thee the best springs; I'll pluck thee berries; 75
I'll fish for thee and get thee wood enough.
A plague upon the tyrant that I serve!
I'll bear him no more sticks, but follow thee,
Thou wondrous man. Wilt thou go with me?

---

[99] siege – excrement, fecal matter
[100] moon-calf – a deformed creature
[101] butt of sack – barrel of Spanish wine

STEPHANO
O brave monster! Lead the way.   80

CALIBAN
(*Sings drunkenly*)
Farewell master; farewell, farewell!
'Ban, 'Ban, Cacaliban
Has a new master: get a new man.
Freedom, hey-day! hey-day, freedom! freedom, hey-day, freedom!

Exeunt

ACT III, SCENE I. Before PROSPERO's cell.
Enter FERDINAND, bearing a log

FERDINAND
There be some sports are painful, and their labour
Delight in them sets off. This my mean[102] task
Would be as heavy to me as odious,[103] but
The mistress which I serve quickens[104] what's dead
And makes my labours pleasures: O, she is   5
Ten times more gentle than her father's crabbed,[105]
And he's composed of harshness. I must remove
Some thousands of these logs and pile them up,
Upon a sore injunction:[106] my sweet mistress
Weeps when she sees me work, and says, such baseness   10
Had never like executor. I forget:
But these sweet thoughts do even refresh my labours,
Most busilest, when I do it.

Enter MIRANDA; and PROSPERO at a distance, unseen

MIRANDA
                    Alas, now, pray you,
Work not so hard: I would the lightning had

---

[102] mean – low, humble
[103] odious – hateful
[104] quickens – to make alive
[105] crabbed – irritable, bad-tempered
[106] sore injunction – evil command, heavy order

Burnt up those logs that you are enjoin'd[107] to pile! 15
Pray, set it down and rest you. My father
Is hard at study; pray now, rest yourself;
He's safe for these three hours.

FERDINAND
                O most dear mistress,
The sun will set before I shall discharge
What I must strive to do.

MIRANDA
                If you'll sit down, 20
I'll bear your logs the while: pray, give me that;
I'll carry it to the pile.

FERDINAND
                No, precious creature;
I had rather crack my sinews, break my back,
Than you should such dishonour undergo,
While I sit lazy by.

MIRANDA
                It would become me 25
As well as it does you: and I should do it
With much more ease; for my good will is to it,
And yours it is against.

PROSPERO
                Poor worm, thou art infected!
This visitation[108] shows it.

MIRANDA
                You look wearily.

FERDINAND
No, noble mistress: 'tis fresh morning with me 30
When you are by at night. I do beseech you –
Chiefly that I might set it in my prayers –
What is your name?

---

[107] enjoin'd – ordered, charged
[108] visitation – a visit

MIRANDA

                      Miranda. – O my father,
I have broke your hest[109] to say so!

FERDINAND

                          Admired Miranda!
Indeed the top of admiration! worth   35
What's dearest to the world! Full many a lady
I have eyed with best regard and many a time
The harmony of their tongues hath into bondage[110]
Brought my too diligent ear: for several virtues
Have I liked several women; never any   40
With so full soul, but some defect in her
Did quarrel with the noblest grace she owed
And put it to the foil:[111] but you, O you,
So perfect and so peerless,[112] are created
Of every creature's best!

MIRANDA

                  I do not know   45
One of my sex; no woman's face remember,
Save, from my glass,[113] mine own; nor have I seen
More that I may call men than you, good friend,
And my dear father: how features are abroad,[114]
I am skilless[115] of; but, by my modesty,   50
The jewel in my dower, I would not wish
Any companion in the world but you,
Nor can imagination form a shape,
Besides yourself, to like of. But I prattle
Something too wildly and my father's precepts[116]   55
I therein do forget.

---

[109] hest – command, order
[110] bondage – servitude
[111] foil – blemish, shortcoming
[112] peerless – unequaled
[113] glass – mirror, looking glass
[114] features are abroad – how people look beyond this island
[115] skilless – ignorant, unacquainted
[116] precepts – instructions, lessons

FERDINAND
                Hear my soul speak:
The very instant that I saw you, did
My heart fly to your service; there resides,
To make me slave to it; and for your sake
Am I this patient log – man.

MIRANDA
                Do you love me?   60

FERDINAND
O heaven, O earth, bear witness to this! I
Beyond all limit of what else i' the world
Do love, prize, honour you.

MIRANDA
                I am a fool
To weep at what I am glad of.

PROSPERO
                Fair encounter
Of two most rare affections! Heavens rain grace   65
On that which breeds between 'em!

FERDINAND
                Wherefore weep you?

MIRANDA
At mine unworthiness that dare not offer
What I desire to give, and much less take
What I shall die to want. But this is trifling;
And all the more it seeks to hide itself,   70
The bigger bulk[117] it shows. Hence, bashful cunning![118]
And prompt me plain and holy innocence!
I am your wife, if you will marry me;
If not, I'll die your maid.

FERDINAND
                My mistress, dearest;
And I thus humble ever.

---

[117] bulk – great size, largeness of the body
[118] bashful cunning – shamefaced falseness

MIRANDA
My husband, then?

FERDINAND
Ay, with a heart as willing
As bondage e'er[119] of freedom: here's my hand.

MIRANDA
And mine, with my heart in't; and now farewell
Till half an hour hence.

FERDINAND
A thousand thousand!

Exeunt FERDINAND and MIRANDA severally

PROSPERO
So glad of this as they I cannot be,
Who are surprised withal. I'll to my book,
For yet ere supper-time must I perform
Much business appertaining.

Exit

ACT III, SCENE II. Another part of the island.
Enter CALIBAN, STEPHANO, and TRINCULO

STEPHANO
My man-monster hath drown'd his tongue in sack. By this light, thou shalt be my lieutenant, monster, or my standard.

TRINCULO
Your lieutenant, if you list; he's no standard.

STEPHANO
Moon-calf, speak once in thy life, if thou beest a good moon-calf.

CALIBAN
How does thy honour? Let me lick thy shoe. I'll not serve him; he's not valiant.

TRINCULO
Thou liest, most ignorant monster. Wilt thou tell a monstrous lie, being but half a fish and half a monster?

---
[119] e'er – ever, at any time

CALIBAN
Lo, how he mocks me! wilt thou let him, my lord?

STEPHANO
Trinculo, keep a good tongue in your head. The poor monster's my subject and he shall not suffer indignity.   10

CALIBAN
I thank my noble lord.

Enter ARIEL, invisible

CALIBAN
As I told thee before, I am subject to a tyrant, a sorcerer, that by his cunning[120] hath cheated me of the island.

ARIEL
Thou liest.

CALIBAN
'Thou liest', thou jesting monkey, thou: I do not lie!   15

STEPHANO
Trinculo, if you trouble him any more in's tale, by this hand, I will supplant[121] some of your teeth.

TRINCULO
Why, I said nothing.

STEPHANO
Mum,[122] then, and no more. Proceed.

CALIBAN
I say, by sorcery he got this isle;   20
From me he got it. If thy greatness will
Revenge it on him, – for I know thou dar'st.
Thou shalt be lord of it and I'll serve thee.

STEPHANO
Canst thou bring me to the party?

---

[120] cunning – art, skill
[121] supplant – displace, remove
[122] mum – an expression implying silence

CALIBAN
Yea, yea, my lord: I'll yield him[123] thee asleep, 25
Where thou mayst knock a nail into his bead.

ARIEL
Thou liest; thou canst not.

CALIBAN
Thou scurvy patch!
I do beseech thy greatness, give him blows.

STEPHANO
Interrupt the monster one word further, and, by this hand – 30

TRINCULO
Why, what did I? I did nothing. I'll go farther off.

STEPHANO
Didst thou not say he lied?

ARIEL
Thou liest.

STEPHANO
Do I so? take thou that.

Beats TRINCULO

As you like this, give me the lie another time. 35

TRINCULO
A pox[124] o' your bottle!

STEPHANO
Stand farther. Come, proceed.

CALIBAN
Why, as I told thee, 'tis a custom with him,
I' th' afternoon to sleep: there thou mayst brain[125] him,
Having first seized his books, or with a log 40
Batter his skull, or paunch[126] him with a stake,

---

[123] yield him – to deliver
[124] pox – used as a slight curse, referring to smallpox
[125] brain – to kill by beating out the brains
[126] paunch – to eviscerate, to rip the belly

Or cut his wezand[127] with thy knife. Remember
First to possess his books; for without them
He's but a sot,[128] as I am, nor hath not
One spirit to command. Burn but his books. 45
He has brave utensils,[129] – for so he calls them –
And that most deeply to consider is
The beauty of his daughter; he himself
Calls her a nonpareil:[130] I never saw a woman,
But only Sycorax my dam[131] and she. 50
Ah, lord; she will become thy bed, I warrant,
And bring thee forth brave brood.[132]

STEPHANO
Monster, I will kill this man: his daughter and I will be
king and queen and Trinculo and thyself shall be viceroys.[133]

ARIEL
This will I tell my master. 55

STEPHANO
Come on, Trinculo, let us sing.

Ariel plays the tune on a tabour and pipe

STEPHANO
What is this same?

TRINCULO
This is the tune of our catch,[134] played by the picture of Nobody.

STEPHANO
If thou beest a man, show thyself in thy likeness: if thou beest
a devil, take't as thou list. 60

CALIBAN
Be not afeard; the isle is full of noises,
Sounds and sweet airs, that give delight and hurt not.

---

[127] wezand – windpipe
[128] sot – blockhead, fool
[129] utensils – anything for daily use, household implements
[130] nonpareil – one who has no equal, a paragon
[131] dam – female parent
[132] brood – the hatch of young, used for men and birds
[133] viceroys – substitute of a king
[134] catch – a song sung in succession

Sometimes a thousand twangling instruments
Will hum about mine ears, and sometime voices
That, if I then had waked after long sleep,   65
Will make me sleep again.

STEPHANO
This will prove a brave kingdom to me, where I shall have my
music for nothing.

CALIBAN
When Prospero is destroyed.

TRINCULO
The sound is going away; let's follow it, and after do our work.   70

Exeunt

ACT III, SCENE III. Another part of the island.
Enter ALONSO, SEBASTIAN, ANTONIO and GONZALO

GONZALO
By'r lakin,[135] I can go no further, sir;
My old bones ache.

ALONSO
              Old lord, I cannot blame thee,
Who am myself attach'd with weariness,
E'en here I will put off my hope: he is drown'd
Whom thus we stray to find. Well, let him go.   5

ANTONIO
(*Aside to SEBASTIAN*) I am right glad that he's so out of hope.
Do not, for one repulse,[136] forego the purpose
That you resolved to effect.

SEBASTIAN
    (*Aside to ANTONIO*) The next advantage
Will we take throughly.

ANTONIO
(*Aside to SEBASTIAN*) Let it be to-night.

---

[135] By'r lakin – a mild oath, byrlady, by our lady-kin
[136] repulse – failure, disappointment

SEBASTIAN
(*Aside to ANTONIO*) I say, to-night: no more. 10

Solemn and strange music

ALONSO
What harmony is this? My good friends, hark!

GONZALO
Marvellous sweet music!

Enter PROSPERO above, invisible. Enter several strange Shapes, bringing in a banquet; they dance about it with gentle actions of salutation; and, inviting the King etc. to eat, they depart

ALONSO
Give us kind keepers, heavens! What were these?

GONZALO
If I should say, I saw such islanders –
For, certes,[137] these are people of the island – 15
Who, though they are of monstrous shape, yet, note,
Their manners are more gentle-kind than of
Our human generation you shall find
Many, nay, almost any.

PROSPERO
   (*Aside*) Honest lord,
Thou hast said well; for some of you there present 20
Are worse than devils.

Thunder and lightning. Enter ARIEL, like a harpy; claps his wings upon the table; and, with a quaint device, the banquet vanishes

ARIEL
You are three men of sin, whom Destiny,
That hath to instrument this lower world
And what is in't, the never-surfeited[138] sea
Hath caused to belch up you; and on this island 25
Where man doth not inhabit; you 'mongst men
Being most unfit to live.

---

[137] certes – certainly
[138] never-surfeited – never nauseous or full to excess

ALONSO, SEBASTIAN, and ANTONIO draw their swords

You fools! I and my fellows
Are ministers of Fate: the elements,
Of whom your swords are temper'd, may as well 30
Kill the still-closing waters, as diminish
One dowle[139] that's in my plume. If you could hurt,
Your swords are now too massy[140] for your strengths
And will not be uplifted. But remember –
For that's my business to you – that you three 35
From Milan did supplant good Prospero;
Exposed unto the sea, which hath requit it,
Him and his innocent child: for which foul deed
The powers, delaying, not forgetting, have
Incensed the seas and shores, yea, all the creatures, 40
Against your peace. Thee of thy son, Alonso,
They have bereft;[141] and do pronounce by me
Lingering perdition, worse than any death
Upon your heads – and nothing but heart-sorrow
And a clear life ensuing. 45

He vanishes in thunder; then, to soft music enter the Shapes again, and dance, with mocks and mows, and carrying out the table

PROSPERO
Bravely the figure of this harpy[142] hast thou
Perform'd, my Ariel. My high charms work
And these mine enemies are all knit up[143]
In their distractions; they now are in my power;
And in these fits I leave them, while I visit 50
Young Ferdinand, whom they suppose is drown'd,
And his and mine loved darling.

Exit above

---

[139] dowle – fiber of down in a feather
[140] massy – heavy
[141] bereft – deprived, stripped
[142] harpy – monster of ancient fables with the face of a woman and the body of a bird
[143] knit up – bound up, tied

GONZALO
I' the name of something holy, sir, why stand you
In this strange stare?

ALONSO
                    O, it is monstrous, monstrous:
Methought the billows spoke and told me of it;   55
That deep and dreadful organ-pipe, pronounced
The name of Prosper: it did bass my trespass.[144]

Exit

SEBASTIAN
But one fiend at a time,
I'll fight their legions o'er.

ANTONIO
                    I'll be thy second.

Exeunt SEBASTIAN and ANTONIO

GONZALO
All three of them are desperate: their great guilt,
Like poison given to work a great time after,
Now 'gins to bite the spirits.

Exit

ACT IV, SCENE I. Before PROSPERO's cell.
Enter PROSPERO, FERDINAND, and MIRANDA

PROSPERO
If I have too austerely punish'd you,
Your compensation makes amends, for I
Have given you here a third of mine own life,
Or that for which I live; who once again
I tender to thy hand: all thy vexations[145]   5
Were but my trials of thy love and thou
Hast strangely stood the test: here, afore Heaven,
I ratify this my rich gift. O Ferdinand,

---
[144] bass my trespass – to announce the crime with a deep voice
[145] vexations – torments, sufferings

Do not smile at me that I boast her off,
For thou shalt find she will outstrip all praise   10
And make it halt behind her.

FERDINAND
                    I do believe it
Against an oracle.

PROSPERO
Then, as my gift and thine own acquisition
Worthily purchased take my daughter: but
If thou dost break her virgin-knot[146] before   15
All sanctimonious[147] ceremonies may
With full and holy rite be minister'd,
No sweet aspersion[148] shall the heavens let fall
To make this contract grow: but barren hate,
Sour-eyed disdain and discord shall bestrew   20
The union of your bed with weeds so loathly
That you shall hate it both: therefore take heed.

FERDINAND
With such love as 'tis now, the murkiest den,
The most opportune place, the strong'st suggestion[149]
Our worser genius can, shall never melt   25
Mine honour into lust, to take away
The edge of that day's celebration.

PROSPERO
Sit then and talk with her; she is thine own.
What, Ariel! my industrious servant, Ariel!

Enter ARIEL

ARIEL
What would my potent master? here I am.   30

PROSPERO
Thou and thy meaner fellows your last service
Did worthily perform; and I must use you

---

[146] virgin-knot – chastity, purity
[147] sanctimonious – outwardly holy
[148] aspersion – sprinkling of dew or rain
[149] suggestion – temptation, seduction

In such another trick. Go bring the rabble,[150]
O'er whom I give thee power, here to this place:
Incite them to quick motion; for I must   35
Bestow upon the eyes of this young couple
Some vanity of mine art.

ARIEL
                    Presently?

PROSPERO
Ay, with a twink.[151]

ARIEL
Before you can say 'come' and 'go',
And breathe twice and cry 'so, so',   40
Each one, tripping on his toe,
Will be here with mop and mow.[152]
Do you love me, master? no?

PROSPERO
Dearly my delicate Ariel. Do not approach
Till thou dost hear me call.

ARIEL
                    Well, I conceive.   45

Exit

PROSPERO
Look thou be true; the strongest oaths are straw
To the fire i' the blood.

FERDINAND
                    I warrant you sir;
The white cold virgin snow upon my heart
Abates the ardour of my liver.

PROSPERO
                    Well.
Now come, my Ariel! appear and pertly!   50

---

[150] rabble – a crowd
[151] twink – in an instant, a twinkling
[152] mop and mow – a grimace, to make faces

No tongue! all eyes! be silent.

Soft music – masque – spirits, etc....

FERDINAND
This is a most majestic vision, and
Harmonious charmingly.[153] May I be bold
To think these spirits?

PROSPERO
                    Spirits, which by mine art
I have from their confines call'd to enact   55
My present fancies.

FERDINAND
                 Let me live here ever;
So rare a wonder'd father and a wife
Makes this place Paradise.

PROSPERO
(*Aside*) I had forgot that foul conspiracy
Of the beast Caliban and his confederates   60
Against my life: the minute of their plot
Is almost come. (*To the Spirits*) Well done! avoid; no more!

FERDINAND
This is strange: your father's in some passion
That works him strongly.

MIRANDA
                 Never till this day
Saw I him touch'd with anger so distemper'd.[154]   65

PROSPERO
You do look, my son, in a moved sort,
As if you were dismay'd: be cheerful, sir.
Our revels now are ended. These our actors,
As I foretold you, were all spirits and
Are melted into air, into thin air: 70
And, like this insubstantial pageant faded,
Leave not a rack[155] behind. We are such stuff

---
[153] charmingly – magically
[154] distemper'd – ill-humored, irritable
[155] rack – floating vapor, a cloud

As dreams are made on, and our little life
Is rounded with a sleep. Sir, I am vex'd;
Bear with my weakness; my, brain is troubled: 75
If you be pleased, retire into my cell
And there repose: a turn or two I'll walk,
To still my beating mind.

FERDINAND and MIRANDA
                        We wish your peace.

Exeunt

PROSPERO
Come with a thought I thank thee, Ariel: come.

Enter ARIEL

ARIEL
Thy thoughts I cleave[156] to. What's thy pleasure?

PROSPERO
                                Spirit, 80
We must prepare to meet with Caliban.
Say again, where didst thou leave these varlets?[157]

ARIEL
I told you, sir, they were red-hot with drinking;
So full of valour…Then I beat my tabour;
And they smelt music: so I charm'd their ears 85
That calf-like they my lowing follow'd through
Tooth'd briers, sharp furzes,[158] pricking goss[159] and thorns,
Which entered their frail shins: at last I left them
I' the filthy-mantled pool beyond your cell.

PROSPERO
This was well done, my bird. 90
Thy shape invisible retain thou still:
For stale[160] to catch these thieves.

---

[156] cleave – abide by, adhere closely
[157] varlets – term of reproach, knave, rascal
[158] furzes – yellow-flowered shrub
[159] goss – shrub with flowers
[160] stale – a decoy, a bait

ARIEL

                I go, I go.

Exit

PROSPERO
I will plague them all,
Even to roaring.

Re-enter ARIEL, with glistering apparel, etc.

                Come, hang them on this line.

PROSPERO and ARIEL remain invisible. Enter CALIBAN, STEPHANO, and TRINCULO, all wet

CALIBAN
This is the mouth o' the cell: no noise, and enter.   95
Do that good mischief which may make this island
Thine own for ever, and I, thy Caliban.

STEPHANO
Give me thy hand. I do begin to have bloody thoughts.

TRINCULO
O King Stephano! O peer! O worthy Stephano! Look what
a wardrobe here is for thee!   100

CALIBAN
Let it alone, thou fool; it is but trash
Let's do the murder first: if he awake,
From toe to crown he'll fill our skins with pinches,
Make us strange stuff.

STEPHANO
Be you quiet, monster. Is not this my jerkin?[161]   105

CALIBAN
I will have none on't: we shall lose our time,
And all be turn'd to barnacles, or to apes.

---

[161] jerkin — a short coat

STEPHANO
Monster: help to bear this away where my hogshead[162] of wine
is, or I'll turn you out of my kingdom: go to, carry this.

TRINCULO
And this. 110

STEPHANO
Ay, and this.

A noise of hunters heard. Enter divers Spirits, in shape of dogs and hounds, hunting them about, PROSPERO and ARIEL setting them on

PROSPERO
Hey, Mountain, hey!

ARIEL
Silver! there it goes, Silver!

PROSPERO and ARIEL
Fury, Fury! there, Tyrant, there! hark! hark! They roar!

CALIBAN, STEPHANO, and TRINCULO are driven out

PROSPERO
Go charge my goblins[163] that they grind their joints. 115
Let them be hunted soundly. At this hour
Lie at my mercy all mine enemies:
Shortly shall all my labours end, and thou
Shalt have the air at freedom: for a little
Follow, and do me service. 120

Exeunt

ACT V, SCENE I. Before PROSPERO's cell.
Enter PROSPERO in his magic robes, and ARIEL

PROSPERO
Now does my project gather to a head:
My charms crack not; my spirits obey; and time
Goes upright[164] with his carriage. How's the day?

---

[162] hogshead – large cask
[163] goblins – mischievous and naughty spirits
[164] goes upright – brings forward all the expected events

ARIEL
On the sixth hour; at which time, my lord,
You said our work should cease.

PROSPERO
                    I did say so,   5
When first I raised the tempest. Say, my spirit,
How fares the King and's followers?

ARIEL
                    Confined together
In the same fashion as you gave in charge,
They cannot budge till your release. The King,
His brother and yours, abide all three distracted   10
And the remainder mourning over them, –
Him that you term'd, sir, 'The good old lord, Gonzalo';
His tears run down his beard, like winter's drops
From eaves of reeds. Your charm so strongly works 'em
That if you now beheld them, your affections   15
Would become tender.

PROSPERO
                    Dost thou think so, spirit?

ARIEL
Mine would, sir, were I human.

PROSPERO
                    And mine shall.
Hast thou, which art but air, a touch, a feeling
Of their afflictions, and shall not myself,
One of their kind, that relish all as sharply,   20
Passion as they, be kindlier[165] moved than thou art?
Though with their high wrongs I am struck to the quick,
Yet with my nobler reason 'gainst my fury
Do I take part: the rarer action is
In virtue than in vengeance. Go release them, Ariel: 25
My charms I'll break, their senses I'll restore,
And they shall be themselves.

---

[165] kindlier – more naturally

ARIEL
                    I'll fetch them, sir.

Exit

PROSPERO
Ye elves of hills, brooks, standing lakes and groves,
And ye that on the sands with printless foot
Do chase the ebbing Neptune and do fly him   30
When he comes back; – I have bedimm'd
The noontide sun, call'd forth the mutinous winds,
And 'twixt the green sea and the azured vault[166]
Set roaring war: to the dread rattling thunder
Have I given fire and rifted[167] Jove's stout oak   35
With his own bolt; the strong-based promontory[168]
Have I made shake and by the spurs pluck'd up
The pine and cedar:
By my so potent Art. But this rough magic[169]
I here abjure,[170] and, when I have required   40
Some heavenly music, which even now I do,
To work mine end upon their senses that
This airy charm is for, I'll break my staff,
Bury it certain fathoms in the earth,
And deeper than did ever plummet sound   45
I'll drown my book.

Solemn music

Enter ARIEL: then ALONSO, with a frantic gesture, attended by GONZALO; SEBASTIAN and ANTONIO in like manner: all enter the circle which PROSPERO had made, and there stand charmed; which PROSPERO observing, speaks:

A solemn air and the best comforter
To an unsettled fancy[171] cure thy brains,
Now useless, boil'd within thy skull! There stand,

---

[166] vault – an arched roof referring to the sky
[167] rifted – cracked, split
[168] strong-based promontory – cape or peninsula standing on a firm foundation
[169] rough magic – sorcery and enchantment that is harsh and rugged of temper
[170] abjure – renounce upon oath
[171] unsettled fancy – disturbed and unhinged imagination

For you are spell-stopp'd. 50
Holy Gonzalo, honourable man,
My true preserver, and a loyal sir
To him you follow'st! I will pay thy graces
Home both in word and deed. Most cruelly
Didst thou, Alonso, use me and my daughter: 55
Thy brother was a furtherer in the act.
Thou art pinch'd[172] fort now, Sebastian. Flesh and blood,
You, brother mine, that entertain'd ambition,
Would here have kill'd your King; I do forgive thee,
Unnatural though thou art. Their understanding 60
Begins to swell, and the approaching tide
Will shortly fill the reasonable shore
That now lies foul and muddy. Not one of them
That yet looks on me, or would know me: Ariel,
Fetch me the hat and rapier in my cell: 65
I will discase[173] me, and myself present
As I was sometime Milan: quickly, spirit;
Thou shalt ere long be free.

ARIEL
(*sings and helps to attire him*)
Where the bee sucks, there suck I:
In a cowslip's[174] bell I lie; 70
There I couch[175] when owls do cry.
On the bat's back I do fly
After summer merrily.
Merrily, merrily shall I live now
Under the blossom that hangs on the bough. 75

PROSPERO
Why, that's my dainty Ariel! I shall miss thee:
But yet thou shalt have freedom: so, so, so.

GONZALO
All torment, trouble, wonder and amazement
Inhabits here: some heavenly power guide us
Out of this fearful country!

---

[172] pinch'd – pained, afflicted
[173] discase – unmask, undress
[174] cowslip – a type of primrose
[175] couch – to lie close and hidden

PROSPERO
                    Behold, sir King,
The wronged Duke of Milan, Prospero:
For more assurance that a living prince
Does now speak to thee, I embrace thy body;
And to thee and thy company I bid
A hearty welcome.

ALONSO
                    Whether thou best he or no,
Or some enchanted trifle to abuse me,
As late I have been, I not know: thy pulse
Beats as of flesh and blood; and, since I saw thee,
The affliction of my mind amends, with which,
I fear, a madness held me: this must crave,
An if this be at all, a most strange story.
Thy dukedom I resign and do entreat
Thou pardon me my wrongs. But how should Prospero
Be living and be here?

PROSPERO
                    First, noble friend,
Let me embrace thine age, whose honour cannot
Be measured or confined.

GONZALO
                    Whether this be
Or be not, I'll not swear.

PROSPERO
                    You do yet taste
Some subtilties[176] o' the isle, that will not let you
Believe things certain. Welcome, my friends all!
(*To ALONSO*) For you, most wicked sir, whom to call brother
Would even infect my mouth, I do forgive
Thy rankest fault; all of them; and require
My dukedom of thee, which perforce,[177] I know,
Thou must restore.

---

[176] subtilties – illusions, deceptions
[177] perforce – yielding to necessity

ALONSO
       If thou be'st Prospero,
Give us particulars of thy preservation; 105
How thou hast met us here, who three hours since
Were wreck'd upon this shore; where I have lost –
How sharp the point of this remembrance is! –
My dear son Ferdinand.

PROSPERO
       I am woe for't, sir:
And have I means much weaker 110
Than you may call to comfort you, for I
Have lost my daughter.

ALONSO
       A daughter?
O heavens, that they were living both in Naples,
The King and Queen there! that they were, I wish.
When did you lose your daughter?

PROSPERO
        In this last tempest. 115
But, howsoe'er you have
Been justled from your senses, know for certain
That I am Prospero and that very duke
Which was thrust forth of Milan, who most strangely
Upon this shore, where you were wreck'd, was landed, 120
To be the lord on't. No more yet of this;
Welcome, sir;
This cell's my court: here have I few attendants
And subjects none abroad: pray you, look in.
My dukedom since you have given me again, 125
I will requite[178] you with as good a thing;
At least bring forth a wonder, to content ye
As much as me my dukedom.

Here PROSPERO discovers FERDINAND and MIRANDA playing at chess

---

[178] requite – repay, reward

MIRANDA
Sweet lord, you play me false.

FERDINAND
                          No, my dear'st love,
I would not for the world.   130

MIRANDA
Yes, for a score of kingdoms you should wrangle,[179]
And I would call it, fair play.

ALONSO
                          If this prove
A vision of the Island, one dear son
Shall I twice lose.

GONZALO
               A most high miracle!

FERDINAND
Though the seas threaten, they are merciful;   135
I have cursed them without cause.

Kneels

ALONSO
                          Now all the blessings
Of a glad father compass thee about!
Arise, and say how thou camest here.

MIRANDA
                          O, wonder!
How many goodly creatures are there here!
How beauteous mankind is! O brave new world,   140
That has such people in't!

PROSPERO
                    'Tis new to thee.

ALONSO
What is this maid with whom thou wast at play?
Your eld'st acquaintance cannot be three hours:

---

[179] wrangle – quarrel, brawl, do wrong to another

Is she the goddess that hath sever'd us,
And brought us thus together?

FERDINAND
                        Sir, she is mortal;   145
But by immortal Providence she's mine:
I chose her when I could not ask my father
For his advice, nor thought I had one. She
Is daughter to this famous Duke of Milan,
Of whom so often I have heard renown,[180]   150
But never saw before; of whom I have
Received a second life; and second father
This lady makes him to me.

ALONSO
              I am hers:
But, O, how oddly will it sound that I
Must ask my child forgiveness!

PROSPERO
                    There, sir, stop: 155
Let us not burthen our remembrance with
A heaviness that's gone.

GONZALO
                I have inly wept,
Or should have spoke ere this. Look down, you gods,
And on this couple drop a blessed crown!
Was Milan thrust from Milan, that his issue[181]   160
Should become Kings of Naples? O, rejoice
Beyond a common joy, and set it down
With gold on lasting pillars.

ALONSO
(*To FERDINAND and MIRANDA*) Give me your hands:
Let grief and sorrow still[182] embrace his heart
That doth not wish you joy!

---

[180] renown – praised
[181] issue – child, children
[182] still – for ever

GONZALO

                Be it so! Amen!   165

ARIEL

(*Aside to PROSPERO*) Sir, all this service
Have I done since I went.

PROSPERO

        (*Aside to ARIEL*) My tricksy[183] spirit!

ALONSO

These are not natural events; they strengthen
From strange to stranger.

ARIEL

  (*Aside to PROSPERO*) Was't well done?

PROSPERO

(*Aside to ARIEL*) Bravely, my diligence.[184] Thou shalt be free.   170
(*To ANTONIO*) Sir, my liege,
Do not infest your mind with beating on[185]
The strangeness of this business; at pick'd leisure
Which shall be shortly single,[186] I'll resolve you,
Which to you shall seem probable, of every   175
These happen'd accidents; till when, be cheerful
And think of each thing well.
(*Aside to ARIEL*) Come hither, spirit:
Set Caliban and his companions free;
Untie the spell.

Exit ARIEL

                How fares my gracious sir?
There are yet missing of your company   180
Some few odd lads that you remember not.

Re-enter ARIEL, driving in CALIBAN

---

[183] tricksy – full of tricks and devices
[184] diligence – constant service and attention
[185] beating on – pondering
[186] shortly single – soon and privately

CALIBAN
O Setebos,[187] these be brave spirits indeed!
How fine my master is! I am afraid
He will chastise me. I shall be pinch'd to death.

PROSPERO
You'd be King o' the isle, sirrah? 185

ALONSO
This is a strange thing as e'er I look'd on.

PROSPERO
He is as disproportion'd in his manners
As in his shape. Go, sirrah, to my cell.

CALIBAN
Ay, that I will; and I'll be wise hereafter
And seek for grace.

PROSPERO
                Go to; away! 190

Exit CALIBAN

PROSPERO
Sir, I invite your highness and your train
To my poor cell, where you shall take your rest
For this one night; which, part of it, I'll waste
With such discourse as, I not doubt, shall make it
Go quick away; the story of my life 195
And the particular accidents gone by
Since I came to this isle: and in the morn
I'll bring you to your ship and so to Naples,
Where I have hope to see the nuptial
Of these our dear-beloved solemnized; 200
And thence retire me to my Milan, where
Every third thought shall be my grave.

ALONSO
                      I long
To hear the story of your life.

---

[187] Setebos – supreme God of the Patagonians, god of Sycorax

PROSPERO
                    I'll deliver all;
And promise you calm seas, auspicious gales,[188]
And sail so expeditious that shall catch[189]
Your royal fleet far off. (*Aside to ARIEL*) My Ariel, chick,
That is thy charge: then to the elements
Be free, and fare thou well! Please you, draw near.

Exeunt

EPILOGUE
Spoken by PROSPERO

Now my charms are all o'erthrown,
And what strength I have's mine own,
Which is most faint: now, 'tis true,
I must be here confined by you,
Or sent to Naples. Let me not,
Since I have my dukedom got
And pardon'd the deceiver, dwell
In this bare island by your spell;
But release me from my bands[190]
With the help of your good hands:
Gentle breath of yours my sails
Must fill, or else my project fails,
Which was to please. Now I want
Spirits to enforce, art to enchant,
And my ending is despair,
Unless I be relieved by prayer,
Which pierces so that it assaults
Mercy itself and frees all faults.
As you from crimes would pardon'd be,
Let your indulgence set me free.

Exit

---

[188] auspicious gales – favorable winds
[189] catch – overtake
[190] bands – fetters, restraints, tethers

10
THE TEMPEST

Suggested cast list and character assignments for a small cast

7 actors, gender flexible. Cast can also be as large as 19 actors.

Actor 1 – Prospero
Actor 2 – Ariel
Actor 3 – Miranda, Mariner (1.1), spirit (3.3)
Actor 4 – Ferdinand, Sebastian
Actor 5 – Alonso, Trinculo, Mariner (1.1), spirit (3.3/4.1)
Actor 6 – Antonio, Caliban, spirit (4.1)
Actor 7 – Gonzalo, Stephano, spirit (4.1)

Alternative cast list for 6 actors* (male or female)

Actor 1 – Prospero, Stephano
Actor 2 – Ariel
Actor 3 – Miranda, Antonio, Mariner (1.1)
Actor 4 – Ferdinand, Sebastian
Actor 5 – Alonso, Trinculo, Mariner (1.1), spirit (3.3/4.1)
Actor 6 – Caliban, Gonzalo, spirit (4.1)

* In 4.1 add a Prospero exit around line 94, Ariel takes Prospero's lines from 112–114, Prospero re-enters at line 115.

* In 5.1 exits for Antonio, Sebastian and Gonzalo will need to be devised so that the actors can then double in the same scene as Miranda, Ferdinand and Caliban.

11
THE WINTER'S TALE

William Shakespeare

Originally written – 1610–1611
First Published – 1623
First recorded performance – 1611

*Edited and Abridged by Julie Fain Lawrence-Edsell
(adapted from http://shakespeare.mit.edu)*

Dramatis Personae

LEONTES, King of Sicilia
CAMILLO, a lord of Sicilia
ANTIGONUS, a lord of Sicilia
POLIXENES, King of Bohemia
FLORIZEL, his son
ARCHIDAMUS, a lord of Bohemia
A Mariner
An old Shepherd, reputed father of Perdita
Clown, his son
~~MAMILLIUS, young Prince of Sicilia~~
~~CLEOMENES, and DION, Lords of Sicilia~~
~~Servant to the old Shepherd~~
~~AUTOLYCUS, a Rogue~~
~~A Gaoler~~

HERMIONE, Queen to Leontes
PERDITA, daughter to Leontes and Hermione
PAULINA, wife to Antigonus
EMILIA, a lady
Other Ladies: attending the Queen
~~MOPSA and DORCAS, Shepherdesses~~
~~Sicilian Lords and Ladies, Attendants, Guards, Satyrs, Shepherds,~~
~~Shepherdesses, &c.~~

Time, as Chorus

ACT I, SCENE I. Antechamber in LEONTES' palace.

Enter CAMILLO and ARCHIDAMUS

ARCHIDAMUS
If you shall chance, Camillo, to visit Bohemia, you shall see
great difference betwixt our Bohemia and your Sicilia.

CAMILLO
I think, this coming summer, the King of Sicilia means to pay
Bohemia the visitation which he justly owes him.

ARCHIDAMUS
Wherein our entertainment shall shame us – 5

CAMILLO
Beseech you, –

ARCHIDAMUS
Verily, I speak it in the freedom of my knowledge: we cannot
with such magnificence, in so rare, I know not what to say. We
will give you sleepy drinks, that your senses, unintelligent of our
insufficience, may, though they cannot praise us, as little accuse us. 10

CAMILLO
You pay a great deal too dear for what's given freely.

ARCHIDAMUS
Believe me, I speak as my understanding instructs me.

CAMILLO
Sicilia cannot show himself over-kind to Bohemia. They were
trained together in their childhoods; and there rooted betwixt
them then such an affection, which cannot choose but branch 15
now. The heavens continue their loves!

ARCHIDAMUS
I think there is not in the world either malice or matter to alter it.

Exeunt

ACT I, SCENE II. A room of state in the same.
Enter LEONTES, HERMIONE, POLIXENES, CAMILLO, and Attendants

POLIXENES
Nine changes of the watery star hath been
The shepherd's note since we have left our throne
Without a burthen: time as long again
Would be fill'd up, my brother, with our thanks.

LEONTES
Stay your thanks a while; 5
And pay them when you part.

POLIXENES
                Sir, that's to-morrow.

LEONTES
One seven-night longer.

POLIXENES
                Very sooth, to-morrow.

LEONTES
We'll part the time between's then; and in that
I'll no gainsaying.[1]

POLIXENES
                Press[2] me not, beseech you, so.
There is no tongue that moves, none, none i' the world, 10
So soon as yours could win me: My affairs
Do even drag me homeward.
Farewell, our brother.

LEONTES
                Tongue-tied, our queen? speak you.

HERMIONE
I had thought, sir, to have held my peace until
You have drawn oaths from him not to stay. You, sir, 15
Charge him too coldly. Tell him, you are sure
All in Bohemia's well.

---

[1] gainsaying – refusing
[2] press – urge

LEONTES
          Well said, Hermione.

HERMIONE
To tell, he longs to see his son, were strong:
But let him say so then, and let him go.
Yet of your royal presence I'll adventure   20
The borrow of a week. When at Bohemia
You take my lord, I'll give him my commission[3]
To let him there a month behind the gest[4]
Prefix'd for's parting: yet – You'll stay?

POLIXENES
                    No, madam.

HERMIONE
Nay, but you will?

POLIXENES
          I may not, verily.   25

HERMIONE
Verily!
You put me off with limber[5] vows; 'Verily,
You shall not go: a lady's 'Verily' 's
As potent as a lord's. Will you go yet?
Force me to keep you as a prisoner,   30
Not like a guest; so you shall pay your fees
When you depart, and save your thanks. How say you?
My prisoner? or my guest? By your dread 'Verily',
One of them you shall be.

POLIXENES
               Your guest, then, madam:
To be your prisoner should import offending;   35
Which is for me less easy to commit
Than you to punish.

HERMIONE
          Not your gaoler,[6] then,
But your kind hostess. Come, I'll question you

---

[3] commission – warrant, power exercised
[4] gest – limited place and time for staying
[5] limber – strengthless, flexible
[6] gaoler – jailer

Of my lord's tricks and yours when you were boys.
You were pretty lordings then?

POLIXENES
                    We were, fair queen,   40

LEONTES
Is he won yet?

HERMIONE
He'll stay my lord.

LEONTES
              At my request he would not.
Hermione, my dearest, thou never spokest
To better purpose.

HERMIONE
              Never?

LEONTES
              Never, but once.

HERMIONE
What! have I twice said well? when was't before?   45
I prithee tell me; cram's with praise to the goal:[7]
My last good deed was to entreat his stay:
What was my first? It has an elder sister,
Nay, let me have't; I long!

LEONTES
              Why, that was when
Three crabbed[8] months had sour'd themselves to death,   50
Ere I could make thee open thy white hand
And clap[9] thyself my love: then didst thou utter
'I am yours for ever'.

HERMIONE
              'Tis grace indeed.
Why, lo you now, I have spoke to the purpose twice:

---

[7] goal – mark, to the purpose
[8] crabbed – morose, miserable, irritated
[9] clap – promise to marry

The one for ever earn'd a royal husband; 55
The other, for some while a friend. (*Giving her hand to Polixenes*)

LEONTES
(*Aside*) Too hot, too hot!
To mingle friendship far is mingling bloods.
I have tremor cordis[10] on me: my heart dances;
But not for joy – not joy. This entertainment 60
But to be paddling palms and pinching fingers,
As now they are, and making practis'd smiles,
My bosom likes not, nor my brows!

POLIXENES
What means Sicilia?

HERMIONE
He something seems unsettled.

POLIXENES
How, my lord! 65
What cheer? how is't with you, best brother?

HERMIONE
You look as if you held a brow of much distraction
Are you moved, my lord?

LEONTES
No, in good earnest.
How sometimes nature will betray its folly,[11]
Its tenderness, and make itself a pastime 70
To harder bosoms! My brother,
Are you so fond of your young prince as we
Do seem to be of ours?

POLIXENES
If at home, sir,
He's all my exercise, my mirth,[12] my matter,
Now my sworn friend and then mine enemy. 75

---

[10] tremor cordis – involuntary and shaking heart
[11] folly – absurdity, weakness of intellect
[12] mirth – merriment

LEONTES

So stands my squire
Officed with me. You two will walk? Hermione,
How thou lovest us, show in our brother's welcome.

HERMIONE

If you would seek us, we are yours i' the garden.

LEONTES

(*Aside*) Go to, go to! 80
How she holds up the neb,[13] the bill[14] to him!
And arms her with the boldness of a wife
To her allowing husband!

Exeunt POLIXENES and HERMIONE

Gone already!
Inch-thick, knee-deep, o'er head and ears a fork'd one![15]
Hermione plays, and I –
Play too, but so disgraced a part, whose issue 85
Will hiss me to my grave. There have been,
Or I am much deceived, cuckolds[16] ere now,
And many a man there is, even at this present,
Now while I speak this, holds his wife by the arm,
That little thinks she has been sluiced[17] in's absence 90
And his pond fish'd by his next neighbour, by
Sir Smile, his neighbor. Should all despair
That have revolted wives, the tenth of mankind
Would hang themselves. Physic[18] for't there is none;
It is a bawdy planet, that will strike 95
It will let in and out the enemy
With bag and baggage – What, Camillo there?

CAMILLO

Ay, my good lord.

---

[13] neb – bill of a bird
[14] bill – mouth of a bird
[15] fork'd one – a horned cuckold
[16] cuckold – man whose wife is false to his bed
[17] sluiced – to make flow as by a floodgate
[18] physic – remedy for a disease

LEONTES
Camillo, this great sir will yet stay longer.

CAMILLO
You had much ado to make his anchor hold.

LEONTES
Didst perceive it? – How came't, Camillo,
That he did stay?

CAMILLO
        At the good queen's entreaty.

LEONTES
At the queen's be't: 'good' should be pertinent
But, so it is, it is not...Ay, but why?

CAMILLO
To satisfy your highness and the entreaties
Of our most gracious mistress.

LEONTES
        Satisfy?
The entreaties of your mistress? Satisfy?
Let that suffice. I have trusted thee, Camillo,
With all the nearest things to my heart, but we have been
Deceived in thy integrity, deceived
In that which seems so.

CAMILLO
        Be it forbid, my lord!

LEONTES
To bide upon't, thou art not honest, or,
If thou inclinest that way, thou art a coward,
A servant grafted[19] in my serious trust
And therein negligent; or else a fool
And takest it all for jest.

CAMILLO
        My gracious lord,
I may be negligent, foolish and fearful;

---

[19] grafted – inserted and rooted for growth

In every one of these no man is free.
If ever I were wilful-negligent,
It was my folly. But, beseech your grace, 120
Be plainer with me; let me know my trespass
By its own visage:[20] if I then deny it,
'Tis none of mine.

LEONTES
              Ha' not you seen, Camillo, –
But that's past doubt, you have, or your eye-glass[21]
Is thicker than a cuckold's horn, – or heard, – 125
My wife is slippery?[22]
My wife's a hobby-horse,[23] deserves a name
As rank as any flax-wench[24] that puts to
Before her troth-plight:[25] say't and justify't!

CAMILLO
I would not be a stander-by to hear 130
My sovereign mistress clouded so, without
My present vengeance taken: 'shrew my heart,
You never spoke what did become you less
Than this; which to reiterate were sin
As deep as that, though true.

LEONTES
              Is whispering nothing? 135
Is leaning cheek to cheek? is meeting noses?
Kissing with inside lip? – is this nothing?
Why, then the world and all that's in't is nothing,
The covering sky is nothing, Bohemia nothing,
My wife is nothing, nor nothing have these nothings, 140
If this be nothing.

CAMILLO
              Good my lord, be cured
Of this diseased opinion, and betimes,
For 'tis most dangerous.

---

[20] visage – face, look
[21] eye-glass – retina, window pane of the eye
[22] slippery – unchaste, immodest, promiscuous
[23] hobby-horse – term of contempt for an unfaithful woman
[24] flax-wench – wanton or lascivious woman
[25] troth-plight – betrothment, formal marriage engagement

LEONTES
                    Say it be, 'tis true.

CAMILLO
No, no, my lord.

LEONTES
                    It is; you lie, you lie:
I say thou liest, Camillo, and I hate thee.   145
Were my wife's liver
Infected as her life, she would not live
The running of one glass.[26]

CAMILLO
                    Who does infect her?

LEONTES
Why, he that wears her like a medal, hanging
About his neck, Bohemia: who, if I   150
Had servants true about me would do that
Which should undo more doing: ay, and thou,
His cupbearer,[27] – whom I from meaner form
Have benched and reared to worship, who mayst see
How I am galled,[28] – mightst bespice[29] a cup,   155
To give mine enemy a lasting wink;
Which draught to me were cordial.[30]

CAMILLO
                    Sir, my lord,
I could do this, and that with no rash potion,
But with a lingering dram that should not work
Maliciously[31] like poison: but I cannot   160
Believe this crack to be in my dread mistress.

LEONTES
Dost think I am so muddy,[32] so unsettled,
To appoint myself in this vexation, sully

---

[26] running of one glass – an hour, flow of sand in an hour glass
[27] cupbearer – conveyer of liquid
[28] galled – injured, annoyed
[29] bespice – poison
[30] cordial – medicinal, reviving the spirits
[31] maliciously – with the strength of hate, harmful, wicked
[32] muddy – disturbed, darkened in the mind

The purity and whiteness of my sheets?
Give scandal to the blood o' the prince my son, 165
Who I do think is mine and love as mine –
Could man so blench?³³

CAMILLO
                    I must believe you, sir:
I do; and will fetch off³⁴ Bohemia for't;
Provided that, when he's removed, your highness
Will take again your queen as yours at first, 170
Even for your son's sake.

LEONTES
                    Thou dost advise me
I'll give no blemish to her honour, none.

CAMILLO
My lord…I am his cupbearer:
If from me he have wholesome beverage,
Account me not your servant.

LEONTES
                    This is all: 175
Do't and thou hast the one half of my heart;
Do't not, thou split'st thine own.

CAMILLO
                    I'll do't, my lord.

LEONTES
I will seem friendly, as thou hast advised me.

Exit

CAMILLO
O miserable lady! But, for me,
What case stand I in? I must be the poisoner 180
Of good Polixenes; and my ground to do't
Is the obedience to a master, one
Who in rebellion with himself will have
All that are his so too. I'd not do't;

---

³³ blench – be inconstant, fly off
³⁴ fetch off – make away with

Let villany itself forswear't. I must
Forsake the court: to do't, or no, is certain
To me a break-neck. Happy star, reign now!
Here comes Bohemia.

Re-enter POLIXENES

POLIXENES
      This is strange: methinks
My favour here begins to warp. Not speak?
Good day, Camillo.

CAMILLO
      Hail, most royal sir!

POLIXENES
What is the news i' the court?

CAMILLO
      None rare, my lord.

POLIXENES
The king hath on him such a countenance
As he had lost some province and a region
Loved as he loves himself: what is breeding
That changes thus his manners.

CAMILLO
I dare not know, my lord.

POLIXENES
Do you know, and dare not? Good Camillo,
Be intelligent to me.

CAMILLO
     There is a sickness
Which puts some of us in distemper, but
I cannot name the disease; and it is caught
Of you that yet are well.

POLIXENES
A sickness caught of me, and yet I well!
I must be answer'd.

CAMILLO
                Sir, I will tell you;
Since I am charged in honour and by him
That I think honourable: therefore mark my counsel,   205
I am appointed him to murder you.

POLIXENES
By whom, Camillo?

CAMILLO
                By the king.

POLIXENES
                For what?

CAMILLO
He thinks, nay, with all confidence he swears,
As he had seen't, that you have touch'd his queen.
Forbiddenly.

POLIXENES
                O, then my best blood turn   210
To an infected jelly and my name
Be yoked[35] with his that did betray the Best![36]
How should this grow?

CAMILLO
I know not: but I am sure 'tis safer to
Avoid what's grown than question how 'tis born.   215
If therefore you dare trust my honesty,
Away to-night! Be not uncertain;
For, by the honour of my parents, I
Have utter'd truth.

POLIXENES
                I do believe thee:
I saw his heart in 's face. Give me thy hand: 220
Be pilot to me – This jealousy
Is for a precious creature: as she's rare,
Must it be great, and as his person's mighty,

---

[35] yoked – joined, coupled
[36] betray the Best – Judas's betrayal of Jesus

Must it be violent. Fear o'ershades me.
I will respect thee as a father if 225
Thou bear'st my life off. Hence! let us avoid.³⁷

CAMILLO
Come, sir, away.

Exeunt

ACT II, SCENE I. A room in LEONTES' palace.
Enter LEONTES, with ANTIGONUS. HERMIONE with her Ladies.

LEONTES
Was he met there? his train? Camillo with him?

ANTIGONUS
Behind the tuft of pines I met them; I eyed them
Even to their ships.

LEONTES
           How blest am I
In my just censure,³⁸ in my true opinion!
Camillo was his help in this, his pander:³⁹ 5
There is a plot against my life, my crown;
All's true that is mistrusted: that false villain
Whom I employ'd was pre-employ'd by him:
Where is my boy: I am glad you did not nurse him:
Though he does bear some signs of me, yet you 10
Have too much blood in him.

HERMIONE
           What is this? sport?⁴⁰

LEONTES
Send the boy hence; he shall not come about her;
Away with him! and let her sport herself
With that she's big with; for 'tis Polixenes
Has made thee swell thus.

---

³⁷ avoid – withdraw, depart
³⁸ censure – judgment, opinion
³⁹ pander – pimp, procurer of prostitutes
⁴⁰ sport – amuse

HERMIONE
       But I'd say he had not,
And I'll be sworn you would believe my saying,
Howe'er you lean to the nayward.[41]

LEONTES
        You, my lords,
Look on her, mark her well; be but about
To say 'she is a goodly lady', and
The justice of your hearts will thereto add
'Tis pity she's not honest, honourable':
She's an adulteress.

HERMIONE
      Should a villain say so,
He were as much more villain: you, my lord,
Do but mistake.

LEONTES
      You have mistook, my lady,
Polixenes for Leontes: O thou thing!
She's an adulteress!

HERMIONE
      Gentle my lord,
You scarce can right me throughly then to say
You did mistake.

LEONTES
      Away with her! to prison!
He who shall speak for her is afar off guilty
But that he speaks.

HERMIONE
      There's some ill planet reigns:
I must be patient till the heavens look
With an aspect more favourable. But I have
That honourable grief lodged here which burns
Worse than tears drown: beseech you all, my lords,
With thoughts so qualified as your charities
Shall best instruct you, measure me; and so
The king's will be perform'd!

---

[41] nayward – opposite side, contradiction

LEONTES
                    Shall I be heard?[42]

HERMIONE
Who is't that goes with me? Beseech your highness,
My women may be with me; for you see
My plight requires it. Do not weep, good fools;   40
There is no cause: when you shall know your mistress
Has deserved prison, then abound in tears.
Adieu, my lord:
I never wish'd to see you sorry; now
I trust I shall. My women, come; you have leave.   45

Exit HERMIONE, guarded; with Ladies

ANTIGONUS
Beseech your highness, call the queen again.
I dare my life lay down and will do't, sir,
Please you to accept it, that the queen is spotless
I' the eyes of heaven and to you –

LEONTES
                    Hold your peace.

ANTIGONUS
You are abused and by some putter-on   50
That will be damn'd for't; would I knew the villain,
I would land-damn[43] him.

LEONTES
                    Cease; no more.
For confirmation, I have dispatch'd in post
To sacred Delphos,[44] to Apollo's temple,
Cleomenes and Dion: now from the Oracle   55
They will bring all;[45] whose spiritual counsel had,
Shall stop or spur[46] me. Have I done well?

---

[42] heard – listened to, obeyed
[43] land-damn – banish from the land
[44] Delphos – thought to be an island, where the oracle of Apollo is
[45] all – the complete truth
[46] spur – hasten, incite

ANTIGONUS
Well done, my lord.

LEONTES
Though I am satisfied and need no more
Than what I know, yet shall the Oracle
Give rest to the minds of others. Come, follow us;
We are to speak in public; for this business
Will raise[47] us all.

ANTIGONUS
        (*Aside*) To laughter, as I take it,
If the good truth were known.

Exeunt

ACT II, SCENE II. A prison.
Enter PAULINA with EMILIA present

PAULINA
Dear gentlewoman,
How fares our gracious lady?

EMILIA
As well as one so great and so forlorn
May hold together: on her frights and griefs,
Which never tender lady hath born greater,
She is something before her time deliver'd.

PAULINA
A boy?

EMILIA
        A daughter, and a goodly babe,
Lusty[48] and like to live: the queen receives
Much comfort in't; says 'My poor prisoner,
I am innocent as you'.

PAULINA
                I dare be sworn
These dangerous unsafe lunes[49] i' the King, beshrew them!
He must be told on't, and he shall: the office

---
[47] raise – rouse, stir, awake
[48] lusty – lively, active, full of spirits
[49] lunes – mad freaks

Becomes a woman best. Pray you, Emilia,
Commend my best obedience to the queen:
If she dares trust me with her little babe, 15
I'll show't the king and undertake to be
Her advocate to the loud'st. We do not know
How he may soften at the sight o' the child.

EMILIA
Most worthy madam,
Your honour and your goodness is so evident 20
That your free undertaking cannot miss
A thriving issue:[50] there is no lady living
So meet for this great errand. I'll presently
Acquaint the queen of your most noble offer;
Now be you blest for it! 25

Exeunt

ACT II, SCENE III. A room in LEONTES' palace.
Enter LEONTES, ANTIGONUS, Lords, and Servants

LEONTES
Fie, fie! Camillo and Polixenes
Laugh at me, make their pastime at my sorrow:
They should not laugh if I could reach them, nor
Shall she, within my power.

Enter PAULINA, with a child

ANTIGONUS
                    You must not enter.

PAULINA
Fear you his tyrannous passion more, alas, 5
Than the queen's life? a gracious innocent soul,
More free than he is jealous.

ANTIGONUS
                    That's enough,
Madam, he hath not slept to-night, commanded
None should come at him.

---
[50] thriving issue – successful event

PAULINA
I come with words as medicinal as true, 10
Honest as either, to purge him of that humour[51]
That presses him from sleep.

LEONTES
Away with that audacious lady! Antigonus,
I charg'd thee that she should not come about me:
I knew she would.

ANTIGONUS
    I told her so, my lord, 15
On your displeasure's peril and on mine,
She should not visit you.

LEONTES
    What, canst not rule her?

PAULINA
From all dishonesty he can:
Good my liege, I come –
And, I beseech you, hear me, who profess 20
Myself your loyal servant, your physician,
Your most obedient counsellor: I say, I come
From your good queen.

LEONTES
    Good queen!

PAULINA
Good queen, my lord, good queen; I say good queen;
And would by combat[52] make her good, so were I 25
A man, the worst about you.

LEONTES
    Force her hence.

PAULINA
Let him that makes but trifles of his eyes
First hand me: on mine own accord I'll off;

---

[51] humour – vanity, change of behavior, conceit
[52] by combat – single fight

But first I'll do my errand. The good queen,
For she is good, hath brought you forth a daughter; 30
Here 'tis; commends it to your blessing.

Laying down the child

LEONTES
                    Out!
A mankind witch! Hence with her, out o' door:
By thy dame Partlet[53] here. Take up the bastard;
Take't up, I say; give't to thy crone.[54]

PAULINA
                    For ever
Unvenerable[55] be thy hands, if thou 35
Takest up the princess by that forced baseness
Which he has put upon't!

LEONTES
                    This brat is none of mine;
It is the issue of Polixenes:
Hence with it, and together with the dam[56]
Commit them to the fire!

PAULINA
                    It is yours; 40
Although the print be little, the whole matter
And copy of the father, eye, nose, lip,
The pretty dimples of his chin and cheek,
The very mould and frame of hand, nail, finger:
So like to him that got it —

LEONTES
                    A gross hag 45
And, lozel,[57] thou art worthy to be hang'd,
That wilt not stay her tongue.

---

[53] dame Partlet – lady
[54] crone – old woman
[55] unvenerable – contemptible, disrespectful
[56] dam – contemptuous word for mother
[57] lozel – coward

ANTIGONUS
                    Hang all the husbands
That cannot do that feat, you'll leave yourself
Hardly one subject.

LEONTES
              I'll ha' thee burnt.

PAULINA
                          I care not:
It is an heretic[58] that makes the fire,   50
Not she which burns in't.

LEONTES
              Away with her!

PAULINA
I pray you, do not push me; I'll be gone.
Look to your babe, my lord; 'tis yours: Jove send her
A better guiding spirit!

Exit

LEONTES
                My child? away with't!
And see it instantly consumed with fire   55
Or I'll seize thy life, Go, take it to the fire;
For thou set'st on thy wife.

ANTIGONUS
                    I did not, sir:
Beseech your highness, give me better credit:
I have always truly served you, and beseech you
On my knees, that you do change this purpose,   60
Which being so horrible, so bloody, must
Lead on to some foul issue.

LEONTES
Shall I live on to see this bastard kneel
And call me father? Better burn it now
Than curse it then. But be it: let it live.   65

---

[58] heretic – a person holding differing opinions from the established faith

To save this bastard's life, – for 'tis a bastard,
So sure as this beard's grey, – what will you adventure
To save this brat's life?

ANTIGONUS
                    Anything, my lord,
I'll pawn[59] the little blood which I have left
To save the innocent: anything possible.   70

LEONTES
It shall be possible. Swear by this sword
Thou wilt perform my bidding.

ANTIGONUS
                    I will, my lord.

LEONTES
Mark and perform it, see'st thou! We enjoin thee,
As thou art liege-man to us, that thou carry
This female bastard hence and that thou bear it   75
To some remote and desert place quite out
Of our dominions, and that there thou leave it,
Without more mercy, to its own protection
Where chance may nurse or end it. Take it up.

ANTIGONUS
I swear to do this, though a present death   80
Had been more merciful. Come on, poor babe:
Some powerful spirit instruct the kites[60] and ravens
To be thy nurses! Sir, be prosperous
In more than this deed does require!
Poor thing, condemn'd to loss!

Exit with the child

LEONTES
                    No, I'll not rear   85
Another's issue.[61]

Exit

---

[59] pawn – assertively defend a position
[60] kites – birds of prey
[61] issue – child

ACT III, SCENE I – cut

ACT III, SCENE II. A court of Justice.
Enter LEONTES, Lords, and Officers

LEONTES
Let us be clear'd
Of being tyrannous, since we so openly
Proceed in justice. Produce the prisoner.

Enter HERMIONE guarded; PAULINA and Ladies attending

LEONTES
Read the indictment.

Officer
(Reads) Hermione, queen to the worthy Leontes, king of Sicilia, thou art here accused and arraigned of high treason, in committing adultery with Polixenes, king of Bohemia, and conspiring with Camillo to take away the life of our sovereign lord the king, thy royal husband.

HERMIONE
Since what I am to say must be but that
Which contradicts my accusation and
The testimony on my part no other
But what comes from myself, it shall scarce boot[62] me
To say 'not guilty': mine integrity
Being counted falsehood, shall, as I express it,
Be so received. You, my lord, best know,
Who least will seem to do so, my past life
Hath been as continent,[63] as chaste, as true,
As I am now unhappy; I appeal
To your own conscience, sir, before Polixenes
Came to your court, how I was in your grace,
How merited to be so.

LEONTES
You will not own it.

---
[62] boot – avail, benefit
[63] continent – free from sexual desire

HERMIONE
                    More than mistress of
Which comes to me in name of fault, I must not
At all acknowledge. For Polixenes,   25
With whom I am accused, I do confess
I loved him as in honour he required,
With such a kind of love as might become
A lady like me, with a love even such,
So and no other, as yourself commanded: 30
Now, for conspiracy: all I know of it
Is that Camillo was an honest man;
And why he left your court, the gods themselves,
Wotting[64] no more than I, are ignorant.

LEONTES
You knew of his departure, as you know   35
What you have underta'en to do in's absence.

HERMIONE
Sir,
You speak a language that I understand not:
My life stands in the level[65] of your dreams,
Which I'll lay down.

LEONTES
                    Your actions are my dreams   40
You had a bastard by Polixenes,
And I but dream'd it! As you – so past all truth,
Shalt feel our justice, in whose easiest passage
Look for no less than death.

HERMIONE
                      Sir, spare your threats:
The bug[66] which you would fright me with I seek.   45
To me can life be no commodity:[67]
The crown and comfort of my life, your favour,
I do give lost; for I do feel it gone,
But know not how it went. My second joy

---

[64] wotting – knowing
[65] level – in the aim of a weapon
[66] bug – bugbear, frightful object
[67] commodity – profit, convenience

And first-fruits of my body, from his presence 50
I am barr'd, like one infectious. My third comfort
Starr'd most unluckily, is from my breast,
The innocent milk in its most innocent mouth,
Haled[68] out to murder: myself on every post
Proclaimed a strumpet: with immodest[69] hatred 55
The child-bed privilege[70] denied, which 'longs[71]
To women of all fashion; lastly, hurried
Here to this place, i' the open air, before
I have got strength of limit. Now, my liege,
Tell me what blessings I have here alive, 60
That I should fear to die? Therefore proceed.
But yet hear this: mistake me not; no life,
I prize it not a straw, but for mine honour,
Which I would free: if I shall be condemn'd
Upon surmises,[72] all proofs sleeping else 65
But what your jealousies awake, I tell you
'Tis rigor[73] and not law. Your honours all,
I do refer me to the Oracle:
Apollo be my judge!

First Lord
                       This your request
Is altogether just: therefore bring forth, 70
And in Apollo's name, his Oracle.

Exit Lord and returns with letter

LEONTES
Break up the seals and read.

Officer
*Hermione is chaste; Polixenes blameless; Camillo a true subject;
Leontes a jealous tyrant; his innocent babe truly begotten; and the
king shall live without an heir, if that which is lost be not found.* 75

---

[68] haled – dragged out
[69] immodest – immoderate, excessive
[70] child-bed privilege – right of a woman in labor
[71] 'longs – belongs
[72] surmises – imagined thoughts, conjectures, suspicions
[73] rigor – cruelty, relentless severity

Lords
Now blessed be the great Apollo!

HERMIONE
                              Praised!

LEONTES
Hast thou read truth?

Officer
                    Ay, my lord; even so –

LEONTES
There is no truth at all i' the Oracle:
The sessions shall proceed: this is mere falsehood.

Enter EMILIA

EMILIA
My lord the King, the King!

LEONTES
                    What is the business?   80

EMILIA
O sir, I shall be hated to report it!
The prince your son, with mere conceit[74] and fear
Of the Queen's speed,[75] is gone.

LEONTES
                    How! gone!

EMILIA
                              Is dead.

LEONTES
Apollo's angry, and the heavens themselves
Do strike at my injustice.

HERMIONE swoons

                    How now there!   85

---

[74] conceit – image, idea, thought
[75] speed – fate, misfortune

PAULINA
This news is mortal to the Queen: look down
And see what death is doing.

LEONTES
                    Take her hence:
Her heart is but o'ercharged; she will recover.
I have too much believed mine own suspicion:
Beseech you, tenderly apply to her   90
Some remedies for life.

Exeunt PAULINA and EMILIA, with HERMIONE

                    Apollo, pardon
My great profaneness 'gainst thine Oracle!
I'll reconcile me to Polixenes,
New woo my queen, recall the good Camillo,
Whom I proclaim a man of truth, of mercy: 95
For being transported by my jealousies
To bloody thoughts and to revenge, I chose
Camillo for the minister to poison
My friend Polixenes: which had been done,
But that the good mind of Camillo tardied   100
My swift command –

Re-enter PAULINA

PAULINA
                    Woe the while!
O, cut my lace, lest my heart, cracking it,
Break too.

LEONTES
            What fit is this, good lady?

PAULINA
What studied torments, tyrant, hast for me?
What wheels? racks? what old or newer torture   105
Must I receive, whose every word deserves
To taste of thy most worst? Thy tyranny
Together working with thy jealousies,

Fancies[76] too weak for boys, too green and idle
For girls of nine, O think what they have done 110
And then run mad indeed, stark mad! for all
Thy by-gone fooleries were but spices[77] of it.
That thou betray'dst Polixenes, 'twas nothing;
That did but show thee, of a fool: nor was't much,
Thou wouldst have poison'd good Camillo's honour, 115
To have him kill a king: poor trespasses,
More monstrous standing by: whereof I reckon
The casting forth to crows thy baby-daughter
To be or none or little;
Nor is't directly laid to thee, the death 120
Of the young prince, so tender, this is not, no,
Laid to thy answer: but the last, – O lords,
When I have said, cry 'woe!' the Queen, the Queen,
The sweet'st, dear'st creature's dead: and vengeance for't
Not dropp'd down yet.

LEONTES
                The higher powers forbid! 125

PAULINA
I say she's dead; I'll swear't. But, O thou tyrant!
Do not repent these things, for they are heavier
Than all thy woes can stir; therefore betake thee
To nothing but despair. A thousand knees
Ten thousand years together, naked, fasting, 130
Upon a barren mountain and still winter
In storm perpetual, could not move the gods
To look that way thou wert.

LEONTES
              Go on, go on
Thou canst not speak too much; I have deserved
All tongues to talk their bitterest.

PAULINA
                  I am sorry for't: 135
I do repent. Alas! I have show'd too much

---

[76] fancies – images, conceptions
[77] spices – only seasoned it

The rashness of a woman: he is touch'd
To the noble heart. Now, good my liege,
Sir, royal sir, forgive a foolish woman:
The love I bore your queen – lo, fool again! –   140
I'll speak of her no more, nor of your children;
I'll not remember you of my own lord,
Who is lost too: take your patience to you,
And I'll say nothing.

LEONTES
                Thou didst speak but well
When most the truth. Prithee, bring me   145
To the dead bodies of my queen and son:
One grave shall be for both: upon them shall
The causes of their death appear, unto
Our shame perpetual. Once a day I'll visit
The chapel where they lie, and tears shed there   150
Shall be my recreation. Come and lead me
Unto these sorrows.

Exeunt

ACT III, SCENE III. Bohemia. A desert country near the sea.
Enter ANTIGONUS with a Child, and a Mariner

ANTIGONUS
Thou art perfect then, our ship hath touch'd upon
The deserts of Bohemia?

Mariner
                Ay, my lord, and fear
We have landed in ill time: the skies look grimly
And threaten present blusters.

ANTIGONUS
                Go, get aboard;
Look to thy bark:[78] I'll not be long before   5
I call upon thee.

---

[78] bark – ship

Mariner
                    Make your best haste, and go not
Too far i' the land: 'tis like to be loud[79] weather;
Besides, this place is famous for the creatures
Of prey that keep upon't.

ANTIGONUS
                    Go thou away:
I'll follow instantly.

Exit

ANTIGONUS
                    Come, poor babe: 10
I have heard, but not believed, the spirits o' the dead
May walk again: if such thing be, thy mother
Appear'd to me last night, in pure white robes,
Like very sanctity, she did approach
My cabin where I lay; thrice bow'd before me,   15
And, gasping to begin some speech, her eyes
Became two spouts: 'Good Antigonus,
Since fate, against thy better disposition,
Hath made thy person for the thrower-out
Of my poor babe, according to thine oath,   20
Places remote enough are in Bohemia,
There weep and leave it crying; and, for the babe
Is counted lost for ever, Perdita,
I prithee, call't'. Blossom, speed thee well!
There lie, and there thy character:[80] there these;[81]   25
Which may, if fortune please, both breed thee, pretty,
And still rest thine. The storm begins; poor wretch,
That for thy mother's fault art thus exposed
To loss and what may follow! Weep I cannot,
But my heart bleeds; and most accursed am I   30
To be by oath enjoin'd to this. Farewell!
The day frowns more and more: I never saw

---

[79] loud – turbulent
[80] character – writing concerning Perdita's name
[81] these – box of gold and jewels

The heavens so dim by day. This is the chase:[82]
I am gone for ever!

Exit, pursued by a bear
Enter a Shepherd

Shepherd
I would there were no age between sixteen and three-and-twenty, 35
or that youth would sleep out the rest; for there is nothing in
the between but getting wenches with child, stealing, fighting –
Hark you now! what have we here! Mercy on 's, a barne a very
pretty barne![83] A boy or a child,[84] I wonder? A pretty one; a very
pretty one: I'll take it up for pity: yet I'll tarry till my son come;
he hallooed but even now. Whoa, ho, hoa! 40

Enter Clown

Clown
Hilloa, loa!

Shepherd
What ailest thou, man?

Clown
I have seen two such sights, by sea and by land!

Shepherd
Why, boy, how is it? 45

Clown
O, the most piteous cry of the poor souls! sometimes to see 'em,
and not to see 'em; now the ship boring[85] the moon with her main-
mast, and anon swallowed with yest and froth.[86] And then for the
land-service,[87] to see how the bear tore out his shoulder-bone;
he cried to me for help and said his name was Antigonus, a how 50

[82] chase – the hunted beast
[83] barne – a little child
[84] child – girl
[85] boring – piercing, penetrating
[86] yest and froth – foam of water
[87] land-service – mischief happening on land

nobleman. But to make anend of the ship, to see how the sea flap-dragoned[88] it: but, first, how the poor souls roared, and the sea mocked them; and how the poor gentleman roared and the bear mocked him, both roaring louder than the sea or weather.

Shepherd
Would I had been by, to have helped the old man! 55

Clown
I would you had been by the ship side, to have helped her.

Shepherd
Heavy matters! heavy matters! but look thee here, boy. Now bless thyself: thou mettest with things dying, I with things new born. Here's a sight for thee; look thee, a bearing-cloth[89] for a squire's[90] child! look thee here; open't. What's within, boy? 60

Clown
Gold! all gold!

Shepherd
This is fairy gold,[91] boy, and 'twill prove so: up with't, keep it close:[92] home, home, the next way.

Clown
Go you the next way with your findings. I'll go see if the bear be gone from the gentleman and how much he hath eaten: if 65 there be any of him left, I'll bury it.

Shepherd
That's a good deed. 'Tis a lucky day, boy, and we'll do good deeds on't.

Exeunt

---

[88] flap-dragoned – swallowed
[89] bearing-cloth – cloth in which a child was carried to the church for baptism
[90] squire – high ranking gentleman, next to a knight
[91] fairy gold – gift from fairies
[92] close – in secret

ACT IV, SCENE I.

Enter Time, the Chorus

Time
I take upon me, in the name of Time,
To use my wings. Impute[93] it not a crime
To me or my swift passage, that I slide
O'er sixteen years since it is in my power
To o'erthrow law and in one self-born hour   5
To plant and o'erwhelm custom. Let me pass.
Your patience this allowing,
I turn my glass and give my scene such growing
As you had slept between: Leontes leaving,
The effects of his fond jealousies so grieving   10
That he shuts up himself, imagine me,
Gentle spectators, that I now may be
In fair Bohemia, and remember well,
I mentioned a son o' the king's, which Florizel
I now name to you; and with speed so pace   15
To speak of Perdita, now grown in grace
Equal with wondering: A shepherd's daughter,
And what to her adheres, which follows after,
Is the argument of Time.

Exit

ACT IV, SCENE II. Bohemia. The palace of POLIXENES.
Enter POLIXENES and CAMILLO

POLIXENES
I pray thee, good Camillo, be no more importunate:[94] 'tis a sickness denying thee anything; a death to grant this.

CAMILLO
It is fifteen years since I saw my country. I desire to lay my bones there. Besides, the penitent[95] king, my master, hath sent for me; to whose feeling sorrows I might be some allay[96] which is another spur to my departure.   5

---
[93] impute – to rate, to account
[94] importunate – urgent
[95] penitent – repentant
[96] allay – that which mitigates and decreases

POLIXENES
As thou lovest me, Camillo, wipe not out the rest of thy services
by leaving me now. Of that fatal country, Sicilia, prithee speak
no more; whose very naming punishes me with the remembrance
of that penitent king, my brother; whose loss of his most pre- 10
cious queen and children are even now to be afresh lamented.
Say to me, when sawest thou the Prince Florizel, my son?

CAMILLO
Sir, it is three days since I saw the prince. What his happier
affairs may be, are to me unknown.

POLIXENES
I have eyes under my service which look upon his removedness; 15
from whom I have this intelligence, that he is seldom from the
house of a most homely shepherd.

CAMILLO
I have heard, sir, of such a man, who hath a daughter of most
rare note.

POLIXENES
That's likewise part of my intelligence. Thou shalt accompany 20
us to the place; where we will, not appearing what we are,
have some question with the shepherd. Prithee, be my present
partner in this business, and lay aside the thoughts of Sicilia.

CAMILLO
I willingly obey your command.

POLIXENES
My best Camillo! We must disguise ourselves. 25

Exeunt

ACT IV, SCENE III – cut

ACT IV, SCENE IV. The Shepherd's cottage.
Enter FLORIZEL and PERDITA

FLORIZEL
These your unusual weeds[97] to each part of you
Do give a life: no shepherdess, but Flora

---
[97] weeds – garments

Peering in April's front. This your sheep-shearing
Is as a meeting of the petty gods,
And you the queen on't.

PERDITA
                    Sir, my gracious lord,
To chide at your extremes[98] it not becomes me:
O, pardon, that I name them! Your high self,
The gracious mark o' the land, you have obscured
With a swain's[99] wearing, and me, poor lowly maid,
Most goddess-like prank'd up:[100] I should blush
To see you so attired, sworn, I think,
To show myself a glass.

FLORIZEL
                  I bless the time
When my good falcon made her flight across
Thy father's ground.

PERDITA
               Now Jove afford you cause!
To me the difference forges dread; your greatness
Hath not been used to fear. Even now I tremble
To think your father, by some accident,
Should pass this way as you did: O, the Fates!
How would he look, to see his work so noble
Vilely bound up? What would he say? Or how
Should I, in these my borrow'd flaunts,[101] behold
The sternness of his presence?

FLORIZEL
                    Apprehend
Nothing but jollity. The gods themselves,
Humbling their deities to love, have taken
The shapes of beasts upon them: Jupiter
Became a bull, and bellow'd; the green Neptune
A ram, and bleated; and the fire-robed god,
Golden Apollo, a poor humble swain,
As I seem now. Their transformations

---

[98] extremes – high passion
[99] swain – peasant, shepherd
[100] prank'd up – dressed up, adorned
[101] flaunts – finery, showy apparel

Were never for a piece of beauty rarer, 30
Nor in a way so chaste.

PERDITA
O, but, sir,
Your resolution cannot hold, when 'tis
Opposed, as it must be, by the power of the king:
One of these two must be necessities,
Which then will speak, that you must change this purpose, 35
Or I my life.

FLORIZEL
Thou dearest Perdita,
With these forced[102] thoughts, I prithee, darken not
The mirth o' the feast. Or I'll be thine, my fair,
Or not my father's. For I cannot be
Mine own, nor any thing to any, if 40
I be not thine. To this I am most constant.
Lift up your countenance, as it were the day
Of celebration of that nuptial which
We two have sworn shall come.

PERDITA
O lady Fortune,
Stand you auspicious![103] 45

Enter Shepherd, Clown, with POLIXENES and CAMILLO disguised

Shepherd
Fie, daughter! when my old wife lived, upon
This day she was both pantler,[104] butler, cook,
Both dame and servant; welcomed all, served all;
Would sing her song and dance – You are retired,
As if you were a feasted one and not 50
The hostess of the meeting: pray you, bid
These unknown friends to's welcome; for it is
A way to make us better friends, more known.
Come, quench your blushes and present yourself
That which you are, mistress o' the feast. 55

---

[102] forced – constrained, far-fetched
[103] auspicious – favorable
[104] pantler – servant in charge of the pantry

PERDITA
(*To POLIXENES*) Sir, welcome:
It is my father's will I should take on me
The hostess-ship o' the day.
(*To CAMILLO*) You're welcome, sir.
For you there's rosemary and rue;[105] these keep   60
Seeming and savour[106] all the winter long:
Grace and remembrance be to you both,
And welcome to our shearing!

POLIXENES
                    Shepherdess,
A fair one are you – well you fit our ages
With flowers of winter.

PERDITA
              Here are flowers   65
Of middle summer, and I think they are given
To men of middle age. You're very welcome.

CAMILLO
I should leave grazing, were I of your flock,
And only live by gazing.

PERDITA
              Out, alas!
You'd be so lean, that blasts of January   70
Would blow you through and through.
(*To FLORIZEL*) Now, my fair'st friend,
I would I had some flowers o' the spring that might
Become your time of day; O, these I lack,
To make you garlands of, and my sweet friend,   75
To strew him o'er and o'er!

FLORIZEL
              What, like a corpse?

PERDITA
No, like a bank for love to lie and play on;
Not like a corpse; or if, not to be buried,
But quick and in mine arms. Come, take your flowers.

---

[105] rue – herb of grace, a symbol of sorry remembrance
[106] savour – smell

FLORIZEL
When you speak, sweet, 80
I'd have you do it ever: when you sing,
I'd have you buy and sell so, so give alms,
Pray so; and, for the ordering your affairs,
To sing them too: when you do dance, I wish you
A wave o' the sea, that you might ever do 85
Nothing but that; But come; our dance, I pray:
Your hand, my Perdita: so turtles[107] pair,
That never mean to part.

PERDITA
           I'll swear for 'em.

POLIXENES
This is the prettiest low-born lass that ever
Ran on the green-sward:[108] nothing she does or seems 90
But smacks of something greater than herself,
Too noble for this place.

CAMILLO
           He tells her something
That makes her blood look out:[109] good sooth, she is
The queen of curds and cream.

FLORIZEL
           Come on, strike up!

Music. Dance of all

POLIXENES
Pray, good shepherd, what fair swain is this 95
Which dances with your daughter?

Shepherd
They call him Doricles; and boasts himself
To have a worthy feeding.[110] He says he loves my daughter:
I think so too; and, to be plain,

---

[107] turtles – turtle doves, who mate for life
[108] green-sward – grassy turf
[109] blood look out – blush
[110] feeding – pasturage, upbringing

I think there is not half a kiss to choose 100
Who loves another best.

POLIXENES
                She dances featly.

Shepherd
So she does any thing; if young Doricles
Do light upon her, she shall bring him that
Which he not dreams of.

POLIXENES
O, father, you'll know more of that hereafter. 105
(*To CAMILLO*) Is it not too far gone? 'Tis time to part them.
He's simple and tells much.
        (*To FLORIZEL*) How now, fair shepherd!
Your heart is full of something that does take
Your mind from feasting.

FLORIZEL
              O, hear me breathe my life
Before this ancient sir! I take thy hand, this hand, 110
As soft as dove's down –

POLIXENES
              What follows this?
How prettily the young swain seems to wash
The hand, was fair before! I have put you out:
But to your protestation; let me hear
What you profess.

FLORIZEL
              Do, and be witness to 't. 115

POLIXENES
And this my neighbour too?

FLORIZEL
              And he, and more
Than he, and men, the earth, the heavens, and all:
That, were I crown'd the most imperial monarch,
Thereof most worthy, I would not prize them
Without her love; for her employ them all. 120

POLIXENES
Fairly offer'd.
CAMILLO
   This shows a sound affection.
Shepherd
But, my daughter,
Say you the like to him?
PERDITA
    I cannot speak
So well, nothing so well; no, nor mean better:
By the pattern of mine own thoughts I cut out   125
The purity of his.
Shepherd
   Take hands, a bargain!
And, friends unknown, you shall bear witness to 't:
I give my daughter to him, and will make
Her portion equal his.
FLORIZEL
   O, that must be
I' the virtue of your daughter: one being dead,   130
I shall have more than you can dream of yet;
Enough then for your wonder. But, come on,
Contract us 'fore these witnesses.
Shepherd
    Come, your hand;
And, daughter, yours.
POLIXENES
   Soft, swain, awhile, beseech you;
Have you a father?
FLORIZEL
   I have: but what of him?   135
POLIXENES
Knows he of this?
FLORIZEL
   He neither does nor shall.

POLIXENES
Methinks a father —
Is at the nuptial of his son a guest
That best becomes the table. Pray you once more,
Is not your father grown incapable   140
Of reasonable affairs? Is he not stupid
With age and altering rheums?[111]

FLORIZEL
                                        No, good sir;
He has his health and ampler strength indeed.

POLIXENES
You offer him, if this be so, a wrong.
The father, all whose joy is nothing else   145
But fair posterity, should hold some counsel
In such a business.

FLORIZEL
                                I yield all this;
But for some other reasons, my grave sir,
Which 'tis not fit you know, I not acquaint
My father of this business.

POLIXENES
                                Let him know't.   150

FLORIZEL
He shall not.

Shepherd
Let him, my son: he shall not need to grieve
At knowing of thy choice.

FLORIZEL
                                Come, come, he must not.
Mark our contract.

POLIXENES
                                Mark your divorce, young sir,

Discovering himself and CAMILLO

---

[111] rheums — rheumatism, inflammation of joints

Whom son I dare not call; thou art too base   155
To be acknowledged: thou a sceptre's[112] heir,
That thus affect'st a sheep-hook! And thou, fresh piece
Of excellent witchcraft, who of force must know
The royal fool thou copest[113] with, —

Shepherd
                        O, my heart!

POLIXENES
I'll have thy beauty scratch'd with briers, and made   160
More homely than thy state. For thee, fond boy,
If I may ever know thou dost but sigh
That thou no more shalt see this knack,[114] as never
I mean thou shalt, we'll bar thee from succession;
Follow us to the court. Thou churl,[115] for this time,   165
Though full of our displeasure, yet we free thee
From the dead blow of it. And you, enchantment, —
Unworthy thee, — if ever henceforth thou
These rural latches to his entrance open,
I will devise a death as cruel for thee   170
As thou art tender to't.

Exit

PERDITA
                Even here undone!
I told you what would come of this: beseech you,
Of your own state[116] take care.

CAMILLO
                        Why, how now, father!
Speak ere thou diest.

Shepherd
                I cannot speak, nor think   175
Nor dare to know that which I know. O sir!
You have undone a man of fourscore three,

---

[112] sceptre — royalty, staff carried as a sign of royalty
[113] copest — encounters
[114] knack — a toy, a petty trifle
[115] churl — peasant, rude and ill-bred fellow
[116] state — station, rank

That thought to fill his grave in quiet, but now…
O cursed wretch,[117]
That knew'st this was the prince, and wouldst adventure 180
To mingle faith with him! Undone! undone!

Exit

FLORIZEL
Why look you so upon me?
I am but sorry, not afeard; delay'd,
But nothing alter'd: what I was, I am.

CAMILLO
Gracious my lord, 185
You know your father's temper: at this time
He will allow no speech, which I do guess
You do not purpose to him;
Then, till the fury of his highness settle,
Come not before him. 190

PERDITA
How often have I told you 'twould be thus!
How often said, my dignity would last
But till 'twere known!

FLORIZEL
                Lift up thy looks:
From my succession wipe me, father; I
Am heir to my affection.

CAMILLO
                Be advised. 195

FLORIZEL
I am, and by my fancy –

CAMILLO
                This is desperate, sir.

FLORIZEL
So call it: but it does fulfil my vow;
I needs must think it honesty. Camillo,

---

[117] wretch – term of contempt, expressing disgust and loathing

Not for Bohemia will I break my oath
To this my fair beloved: therefore, I pray you, 200
As you have ever been my father's honour'd friend,
When he shall miss me, cast your good counsels –
And so deliver, I am put to sea
With her whom here I cannot hold on shore;
What course I mean to hold 205
Shall nothing benefit your knowledge –

CAMILLO
                              My lord,
I would your spirit were easier[118] for advice.

FLORIZEL
Hark, Perdita (*Drawing her aside*)
(*To CAMILLO*) I'll hear you by and by.

CAMILLO
                          He's irremoveable,
Resolved for flight. Now were I happy, if 210
His going I could frame to serve my turn,
Save him from danger, do him love and honour,
Purchase the sight again of dear Sicilia
And that unhappy king, my master, whom
I so much thirst to see.

FLORIZEL
                    Now, good Camillo. 215

CAMILLO
If you may please to think I love the king
And through him what is nearest to him, which is
Your gracious self, embrace but my direction:
I'll point you where you shall have such receiving
As shall become your highness – make for Sicilia, 220
And there present yourself and your fair princess,
For so I see she must be, 'fore Leontes:
Methinks I see –
Leontes opening his free arms and weeping
His welcomes forth; asks thee there 'Son forgiveness', 225
As 'twere i' your father's person.

---

[118] easier – willingly open

FLORIZEL
                              Worthy Camillo,
What colour[119] for my visitation shall I
Hold up before him?

CAMILLO
                    Sent by the king your father
To greet him and to give him comforts, Sir,
And speak his very heart.

FLORIZEL
                    I am bound to you:
But O, the thorns we stand upon! Camillo,
Preserver of my father, now of me.
We are not furnish'd[120] like Bohemia's son,
Nor shall appear in Sicilia.

CAMILLO
                    My lord,
Fear none of this: I think you know my fortunes
Do all lie there: it shall be so my care
To have you royally appointed.
And, but my letters, by this means being there
So soon as you arrive, shall clear all doubt.

FLORIZEL
And those that you'll procure from King Leontes –

CAMILLO
Shall satisfy your father.

PERDITA
                    Happy be you!
All that you speak shows fair.

FLORIZEL
                    Fortune speed us!
Thus we set on, Camillo, to the sea-side.

CAMILLO
The swifter speed the better.
(*Aside*) What I do next, shall be to tell the king
Of this escape and whither they are bound;

---

[119] colour – appearance of right, superficial posturing
[120] furnish'd – equipped, supplied

Wherein my hope is I shall so prevail
To force him after: in whose company
I shall review Sicilia!

Exeunt FLORIZEL, PERDITA, and CAMILLO
Re-enter Clown and Shepherd

Clown
See, see; what a man you are now! There is no other way but to   250
tell the king she's a changeling[121] and none of your flesh and
blood; and so your flesh and blood is not to be punished by
him. Show those things you found about her, those secret
things, this being done, let the law go whistle:[122] I warrant you.

Shepherd
I will tell the king all, every word, yea, and his son's pranks   255
too; to go about to make me the king's brother-in-law.

Clown
Indeed, brother-in-law!

Shepherd
Well, let us to the king: there is that in this fardel[123] will make
him scratch his beard.

Clown
We must to the king and show our strange sights.   260

Exit

ACT V, SCENE I. A room in LEONTES' palace.
Enter LEONTES, PAULINA, and Servants

PAULINA
Sir, you have done enough, and have perform'd
A saint-like sorrow: no fault could you make,
Which you have not redeem'd; indeed, paid down
More penitence than done trespass:[124] at the last,
Do as the heavens have done, forget your evil;   5
With them forgive yourself.

---

[121] changeling – a child left or taken by the fairies
[122] whistle – i.e. beyond the reach of it, also – to make a shrill sound
[123] fardel – pack, bundle
[124] trespass – offence, sin

LEONTES
                    Whilst I remember
Her and her virtues, I cannot forget
My blemishes[125] in them, and so still think of
The wrong I did myself; which was so much,
That heirless it hath made my kingdom and   10
Destroy'd the sweet'st companion that e'er man
Bred[126] his hopes out of.

PAULINA
                    True, too true, my lord:
If, one by one, you wedded all the world,
Or from the all that are took something good,
To make a perfect woman, she you kill'd   15
Would be unparallel'd.

LEONTES
                    I think so. Kill'd!
She I kill'd! I did so: but thou strikest me
Sorely, to say I did; O Good Paulina,
Who hast the memory of Hermione,
I know, in honour, O, that ever I   20
Had squared[127] me to thy counsel! Then, even now,
I might have look'd upon my queen's full eyes,
Have taken treasure from her lips, –

PAULINA
                    And left them
More rich for what they yielded.

LEONTES
                    Thou speak'st truth.
No more such wives; therefore, no wife.   25

PAULINA
Were I the ghost that walk'd, I'd bid you mark[128]
Her eye, and tell me for what dull part in't
You chose her; then I'd shriek, that even your ears

---

[125] blemishes – disfigures, stains
[126] bred – produced
[127] squared – adjusted, regulated, shaped
[128] mark – observe

Should rift[129] to hear me; and the words that follow'd
Should be 'Remember mine'.

LEONTES
                          Fear thou no wife;
I'll have no wife, Paulina.

PAULINA
                Will you swear
Never to marry but by my free leave?

LEONTES
Never, Paulina; so be blest my spirit!

PAULINA
Yet, if my lord will marry, – give me the office
To choose you a queen: she shall not be so young
As was your former; but she shall be such
As, walk'd your first queen's ghost, it should take joy
To see her in your arms.

LEONTES
                    My true Paulina,
We shall not marry till thou bid'st us.

PAULINA
                        That
Shall be when your first queen's again in breath;
Never till then.

Enter a Gentleman

Gentleman
One that gives out himself Prince Florizel,
Son of Polixenes, with his princess, she
The fairest I have yet beheld, desires access
To your high presence.

LEONTES
                What with him? his approach,
So out of circumstance and sudden, tells us

---

[129] rift – to burst, to be split

'Tis not a visitation framed,[130] but forced
By need and accident.
His princess, say you, with him?

Gentleman
Ay, the most peerless[131] piece of earth, I think,
That e'er the sun shone bright on.

PAULINA
                  O Hermione,
Give way to what's seen now! Sir, you yourself
Have said and writ so, but your writing now
Is colder than that theme, 'She had not been,
Nor was not to be equall'd'; –

Gentleman
                  Pardon, madam:
The one I have almost forgot, – your pardon, –

LEONTES
Bring them to our embracement. Still, 'tis strange
He thus should steal upon us.

PAULINA
                  Had our prince,
Jewel of children, seen this hour, he had pair'd
Well with this lord: there was not full a month
Between their births.

LEONTES
Prithee, no more; cease; thou know'st
He dies to me again when talk'd of:
They are come.

Enter FLORIZEL and PERDITA

Your mother was most true to wedlock,[132] prince;
For she did print your royal father off,
Conceiving you: were I but twenty-one,
Your father's image is so hit in you,
That I should call you brother. Most dearly welcome!

---
[130] framed – planned
[131] peerless – unequaled
[132] wedlock – ceremony of being married

And your fair princess, – goddess! – O, alas! 70
I lost a couple, that 'twixt heaven and earth
Might thus have stood begetting wonder as
You, gracious couple, do: and then I lost –
All mine own folly – the society,
Amity too, of your brave father, whom, 75
Though bearing misery, I desire my life
Once more to look on him.

FLORIZEL
                    By his command
Have I here touch'd Sicilia and from him
Give you all greetings that a king, at friend,
Can send his brother: whom he loves – 80
He bade me say so – more than all the sceptres
And those that bear them living.

LEONTES
                    O my brother,
Good gentleman! the wrongs I have done thee stir
Afresh within me. You have a holy father,
A graceful gentleman; against whose person, 85
So sacred as it is, I have done sin:
For which the heavens, taking angry note,
Have left me issueless.[133] What might I have been,
Might I a son and daughter now have look'd on,
Such goodly things as you!

Enter a Lord

Lord
                    Most noble sir, 90
That which I shall report will bear no credit,
Were not the proof so nigh.[134] Please you, great sir,
Bohemia greets you from himself by me;
Desires you to attach[135] his son, who has –
His dignity and duty both cast off – 95
Fled from his father, from his hopes, and with
A shepherd's daughter.

[133] issueless – without children or an heir
[134] nigh – near
[135] attach – seize

LEONTES
                    Where's Bohemia? speak.

Lord
Here in your city; I now came from him,
Whiles he was hastening, in the chase, it seems,
Of this fair couple.

FLORIZEL
                    Camillo has betray'd me;   100
Whose honour and whose honesty till now
Endured all weathers.

Lord
                    Lay't so to his charge:[136]
He's with the king your father.

LEONTES
                    Who? Camillo?

Lord
Camillo, sir; I spake with him.

Exit Lord

PERDITA
The heaven sets spies upon us, will not have   105
Our contract celebrated.

LEONTES
                    You are married?

FLORIZEL
We are not, sir, nor are we like to be.

LEONTES
                                My lord,
Is this the daughter of a king?

FLORIZEL
                        She is,
When once she is my wife.

---

[136] charge — order, office

LEONTES
That 'once' I see by your good father's speed   110
Will come on very slowly. I am sorry,
Most sorry, you have broken from his liking
Where you were tied in duty, and as sorry
Your choice is not so rich in worth as beauty,
That you might well enjoy her.

FLORIZEL
                        Dear, look up: 115
Though Fortune,[137] visible an enemy,
Should chase us with my father, power no jot[138]
Hath she to change our loves. Beseech you, sir,
Remember since you owed no more[139] to time
Than I do now: with thought of such affections,   120
Step forth mine advocate; at your request
My father will grant precious things as trifles.

LEONTES
Would he do so, I'd beg your precious mistress,
Which he counts but a trifle.

PAULINA
                Sir, my liege,
Your eye hath too much youth in't: not a month   125
'Fore[140] your queen died, she was more worth such gazes
Than what you look on now.

LEONTES
                I thought of her,
Even in these looks I made. (*To FLORIZEL*) But your petition
Is yet unanswer'd. I will to your father:
Your honour not o'erthrown[141] by your desires,   130
I am friend to them and you: therefore follow me
And mark what way I make: come, good my lord.

Exeunt

---

[137] Fortune – the goddess, bringing good or ill luck
[138] jot – least quantity imaginable
[139] owed no more – were at the same age
[140] 'fore – before
[141] honour not o'erthrown – love is honorable

ACT V, SCENE II. Before LEONTES' palace.

Enter Lord and two Gentleman

Lord
Beseech you, sir, were you present at this relation?

First Gentleman
I was by at the opening of the fardel, heard the old shepherd deliver the manner how he found it: whereupon, after a little amazedness, I heard the shepherd say, he found the child.

Second Gentleman
The Oracle is fulfilled; the king found his heir! The mantle[142] of Queen Hermione's, her jewel about the neck of it, the letters of Antigonus found with it, the majesty of the creature in resemblance of the mother and many other evidences proclaim her with all certainty to be the king's daughter. Our king, being ready to leap out of himself for joy cries 'O, thy mother, thy mother!' then asks Bohemia forgiveness; then embraces his son-in-law. But O, the noble Paulina! She had one eye declined for the loss of her husband, another elevated that the Oracle was fulfilled: she lifted the princess from the earth, and so locks her in embracing. 5

10

First Gentleman
Are they returned to the court? 15

Second Gentleman
No, the princess hearing of her mother's statue, which is in the keeping of Paulina, – a piece many years in doing and so near to Hermione that they say one would speak to her and stand in hope of answer: thither with all greediness of affection are they gone.

First Gentleman
Let's along. 20

Exeunt Gentlemen

---

[142] mantle – cloak

ACT V, SCENE III. A chapel in PAULINA's house.

Enter LEONTES, POLIXENES, FLORIZEL, PERDITA, CAMILLO, and PAULINA

LEONTES
O grave and good Paulina, the great comfort
That I have had of thee!

PAULINA
     What, sovereign sir,
I did not well I meant well. All my services
You have paid home:[143] my poor house to visit,
It is a surplus of your grace, which never   5
My life may last to answer.

LEONTES
     O Paulina,
We honour you with trouble: but we came
To see the statue of our queen.

PAULINA
     As she lived peerless,
So her dead likeness, I do well believe,
Excels whatever yet you look'd upon   10
Or hand of man hath done. But here it is: prepare
To see the life as lively mock'd[144] as ever,
Behold, and say 'tis well.

PAULINA draws a curtain, and discovers HERMIONE standing like a statue

I like your silence, it the more shows off
Your wonder: but yet speak; first, you, my liege.   15
Comes it not something near?

LEONTES
     Her natural posture!
Chide me, dear stone, that I may say indeed
Thou art Hermione. But yet, Paulina,

---

[143] paid home – to give in requite for a wrongdoing
[144] lively mocked – naturally imitated, life-like

Hermione was not so much wrinkled, nothing
So aged as this seems.

POLIXENES
                O, not by much.

PAULINA
So much the more our carver's excellence;
Which lets go by some sixteen years and makes her
As she lived now.

LEONTES
               As now she might have done,
So much to my good comfort, as it is
Now piercing[145] to my soul. O, thus she stood,
Even with such life of majesty, warm life,
As now it coldly stands, when first I woo'd[146] her!
I am asham'd. O royal piece,
There's magic in thy majesty.

PERDITA
                 Lady,
Dear queen, that ended when I but began,
Give me that hand of yours to kiss.

PAULINA
                 O, patience!
The statue is but newly fix'd,[147] the colour's
Not dry.

CAMILLO
My lord, your sorrow was too sore[148] laid on,[149]
Which sixteen winters cannot blow away,
So many summers dry.

POLIXENES
             Dear my brother,
Let him that was the cause of this have power

---

[145] piercing – affecting deeply
[146] woo'd – to court, to solicit in love
[147] fix'd – painted
[148] sore – grievously, heavily
[149] laid on – exhibited, displayed

To take off so much grief from you as he
Will piece up[150] in himself.

PAULINA
                    Indeed, my lord,
If I had thought the sight of my poor image   40
Would thus have wrought[151] you, – for the stone is mine –
I'd not have show'd it.

LEONTES
                    Do not draw the curtain.

PAULINA
No longer shall you gaze on't, lest your fancy
May think anon it moves.

LEONTES
                    See, my lord,
Would you not deem it breathed? and that those veins   45
Did verily bear blood?

POLIXENES
                    Masterly done:
The very life seems warm upon her lip.

LEONTES
The fixture of her eye has motion in't,
As we are mock'd with art.

PAULINA
                    I'll draw the curtain:
My lord's almost so far transported that   50
He'll think anon it lives.

LEONTES
                    O sweet Paulina,

PAULINA
I am sorry, sir, I have thus far stirr'd you –

LEONTES
                    Methinks
There is an air comes from her: what fine chisel

---
[150] piece up – make full, supply
[151] wrought – produced, acted upon

Could ever yet cut breath? Let no man mock me,
For I will kiss her.

PAULINA
                    Good my lord, forbear:[152]
Quit presently the chapel, or resolve[153] you
For more amazement. If you can behold it,
I'll make the statue move indeed,[154] descend
And take you by the hand.

LEONTES
                    What you can make her do,
I am content to look on: what to speak,
I am content to hear.

PAULINA
                    It is required
You do awake your faith. Then all stand still;
Or, those that think it is unlawful business
I am about, let them depart.

LEONTES
                    Proceed:
No foot shall stir.

PAULINA
                    Music, awake her; strike!

Music

'Tis time; descend; be stone no more; approach;
Strike all that look upon with marvel. Come,
I'll fill your grave up: stir, nay, come away,
Bequeath[155] to death your numbness, for from him
Dear life redeems you. You perceive she stirs:

HERMIONE comes down

---

[152] forbear – stop doing what was purposed, abstain
[153] resolve – prepare
[154] indeed – in reality
[155] bequeath – yield, bestow upon

Start[156] not; her actions shall be holy as
You hear my spell is lawful: do not shun[157] her
Until[158] you see her die again; for then
You kill her double. Nay, present your hand:
When she was young you woo'd her; now in age   75
Is she become the suitor?

LEONTES
                O, she's warm!

POLIXENES
She embraces him.

CAMILLO
                She hangs about his neck:
If she pertain to life[159] let her speak too.

POLIXENES
Or how stolen from the dead.

PAULINA
                That she is living,
Were it but told you, should be hooted[160] at   80
Like an old tale: but it appears she lives,
Though yet she speak not. Mark a little while.
(*To PERDITA*) Please you to interpose, fair madam: kneel
And pray your mother's blessing. (*To HERMIONE*) Turn,
    good lady;
Our Perdita is found.

HERMIONE
              You gods, look down   85
And from your sacred vials pour your graces
Upon my daughter's head! Tell me, mine own.
Where hast thou been preserved? where lived? how found
Thy father's court? for thou shalt hear that I,
Knowing by Paulina that the Oracle   90

---

[156] start – make a sudden and involuntary motion, twitch
[157] shun – avoid, keep far from
[158] until – till, up to the time
[159] pertain to life – if she lives
[160] hooted – shout with contempt

Gave hope thou wast in being, have preserved
Myself to see the issue.[161]

PAULINA
                    Go together,
You precious winners all; your exultation
Partake to[162] every one. I, an old turtle,
Will wing me to some wither'd bough and there   95
My mate, that's never to be found again,
Lament, till I am lost.[163]

LEONTES
                    O, peace, Paulina!
Thou shouldst a husband take by my consent,
As I by thine a wife: this is a match,
And made between's by vows. Thou hast found mine;   100
But how, is to be question'd; for I saw her,
As I thought, dead, and have in vain said many
A prayer upon her grave. I'll not seek far –
For him, I partly know his mind – to find thee
An honourable husband. Come, Camillo,   105
And take her by the hand, whose worth and honesty
Is richly noted and here justified[164]
By us, a pair of kings. Let's from this place.
(*To HERMIONE*) What! look upon my brother: both your pardons,
That e'er I put between your holy looks   110
My ill suspicion. This is your son-in-law,
And son unto the king, who, heavens directing,
Is troth-plight[165] to your daughter. Good Paulina,
Lead us from hence, where we may leisurely
Each one demand an answer to his part   115
Perform'd in this wide gap of time since first
We were dissever'd:[166] hastily lead away.

Exeunt

---

[161] issue – final event
[162] partake to – communicate
[163] lost – dead, gone
[164] justified – confirmed what is declared, ratified
[165] troth-plight – betrothed, engaged to
[166] dissever'd – separated

12
THE WINTER'S TALE

Suggested cast list and character assignments for a small cast

<u>7 actors, gender flexible. Cast can also be as large as 19 actors.</u>

    Actor 1 – Leontes, Old Shepherd
    Actor 2 – Polixenes, Antigonus
    Actor 3 – Camillo, Mariner, Gentleman (5.1), Lord (5.2)
    Actor 4 – Hermione, Clown
    Actor 5 – Paulina, Time
    Actor 6 – Perdita, Emilia, First Gentleman (5.2)
    Actor 7 – Florizel, Archidamus, Officer (3.2), Second Gentleman (5.2)

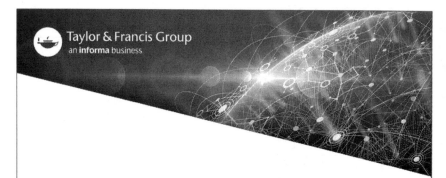

Taylor & Francis eBooks

www.taylorfrancis.com

A single destination for eBooks from Taylor & Francis with increased functionality and an improved user experience to meet the needs of our customers.

90,000+ eBooks of award-winning academic content in Humanities, Social Science, Science, Technology, Engineering, and Medical written by a global network of editors and authors.

TAYLOR & FRANCIS EBOOKS OFFERS:

- A streamlined experience for our library customers
- A single point of discovery for all of our eBook content
- Improved search and discovery of content at both book and chapter level

REQUEST A FREE TRIAL
support@taylorfrancis.com